10 Minute Guide to Planning

by Edwin E. Bobrow, CMC, CPMC

alpha books

Macmillan Spectrum/Alpha Books

A Division of Macmillan General Reference
A Simon and Schuster Macmillan Company
1633 Broadway, New York, NY 10019-6785

Macmillan Publishing books may be purchased for business or sales promotional use. For information please write: Special Markets Department, Macmillan Publishing USA, 1633 Broadway, New York, NY 10019.

International Standard Book Number: 0-02-861818-1

Library of Congress Catalog Card Number: 97-071161

00 99 98 8 7 6 5 4 3 2

Interpretation of the printing code: the rightmost double-digit number is the year of the book's first printing; the rightmost single-digit number is the number of the book's printing. For example, a printing code of 98-1 shows that this copy of the book was printed during the first printing of the book in 1998.

Printed in the United States of America

Publisher: Kathy Nebenhaus

Managing Editor: Bob Shuman

Production Editors: Mark Enochs, Jessica Ford

Copy Editor: Erik Dafforn

Cover Designer: Dan Armstrong

Designer: Glenn Larsen

Indexer: Ginny Bess

Production Team: Angela Calvert, Kim Cofer, Nicole Ritch, Scott Tullis

Contents

Introduction

Too often our lives and work activities are left to flounder on a sea of luck and opportunity. Planning takes your life and your organization's life and gives it strategic direction. It helps you determine: *where* you want to go; *how* you will get there; *what* you'll do to achieve it; *who* will help you get there; and, through scheduling, *when* you will arrive. Without going through the planning process it is difficult—if not impossible—to take charge of your destiny and your organization's destiny.

Don't be afraid to plan. It is not complicated and it is often easy to do. Like any other good habit, you just have to start doing it and it will stay with you forever. It is what helps you become a strategic thinker and, most important, it will help you:

- Develop a clear vision of what you or your organization sees for the future.
- Establish the mission of getting what is wanted.
- Develop specific goals or objectives.
- Set the strategies of how you will achieve your goals.
- Build a schedule for when it will all happen.
- Establish what success will be and how to measure it.

Don't make the mistake of thinking you can plan in your head. For planning to have any value it must be written down. Only by writing each step and then writing the final plan can you see where you are going. Similarly, it also enables you to look back to determine if you have done what you planned to do.

Now, use this 10 Minute Guide to help take you through both the genteel and rough seas out there so you can reach your objectives when you want to and in the most direct manner.

CONVENTIONS USED IN THIS BOOK

In this book, there are three types of icons to help you locate important information:

Tip These icons provide ideas that help you cut corners and avoid confusion.

Plain English These icons are shown to define new terms.

Panic Button These icons point out potential problems and offer solutions to them.

THE AUTHOR

Edwin E. Bobrow, CMC*, CPCM**, is president of his 29-year-old consulting company and is an adjunct associate professor at New York University, The Marketing and Management Institute. He teaches and lectures on strategic planning, consulting skills and practice, new product development, selling through independent reps, and basic marketing. Professor

Bobrow is an international lecturer and businessperson who has written seven books and co-edited three. He has also written over 125 articles on planning, management, and marketing.

** Certified Management Consultant*

***Certified Professional Consultant to Management*

E-Mail: **EdBobrow@Compuserve.com**
Web Address: **http://www.mcninet.com/GlobalLOOK/edbobrow.html**

LESSON 1

Planning Starts with Personal Planning

In this lesson you gain an understanding of the importance of personal planning and how it relates to successful business planning.

What Is Planning and Scheduling?

Planning is like pulling the five fingers of your hand into a fist and directing it toward what you want to achieve—your goals or aims. If you try to strike with just one extended finger at a time, it will fold as pressure is applied. But if you pull those fingers into a fist you will have impact in whatever direction you aim that fist.

If you assemble your resources or your company resources into a fist, it will impact where you direct it, toward your goals or aims. That, after all, defines planning—assembling all of those resources to achieve your aims or goals and to develop clear actions or strategies in order to achieve them. Scheduling is setting timeframes for when the actions will happen along the way to implement and complete your plan.

Plan A method for achieving an end.

Scheduling Setting a timetable as to when things will happen.

WHY IS PERSONAL PLANNING IMPORTANT?

Once, when I gave a seminar on planning for the Sales and Marketing Executives of Greater New York, a husband and wife owner of a small chain of furniture stores brought up the problems of planning for their business. Should they open more stores? Where should the stores be opened? Should they sell most of the stores? Would it be better to have one giant store and fewer small stores? There was a "eureka" expression on their face when I asked them what they wanted out of life. Did they want to make a lot of money? Did they want to spend most of their time working? Ideally where would they like to live? And so on. In other words, had they done any personal planning? Had they looked into their feelings and desires? For these two owners, as with most all entrepreneurs, what they want out of life should be reflected in their business planning.

Getting There Is Half the Fun When you're doing what you planned in order to achieve your dreams you will be a happy person.

Those who choose to go through life rudderless—that is, without planning, are usually powerless. To choose where you will go with your life and how you will get there, you need clear goals (end aims) and strategies or actions (how you will achieve the end aims). Only then will you have the power to direct your life and to marshal your personal resources productively. Whether or not you are aware of your goals and strategies, they are steering your life. But when you bring them into full consciousness, through planning, you become the captain who steers your life successfully.

As the baseball immortal Casey Stengel said, "If you don't know where you're going, you may end up somewhere else." Who wants to wind up somewhere else? We all want to wind up in the place that our personal vision dictates. Yet, how many of us have defined our personal vision, let alone our vision of where we want to go with a business? If indeed we do have a clear vision, then we can draw a map that will get us there and not somewhere else.

Don't Count on Your Memory If you don't write down your vision you may lose it.

In order to reach the places in life that you want to be you must assemble into your plan the business aspects of your life as well as the various non-business aspects. If, for example, you want to work toward establishing your own business, you have to weigh and plan the actions needed to achieve it against all else that will affect your business actions. You might be sacrificing the amount of time you spend with your family, risk security for uncertainty, give up the comfort of following for the exultation of leading, have less vacation or travel time, and so on. Conversely, if your plan is to achieve a certain level within your company, you may be sacrificing freedom of independent action or the chance to own your business for benefits such as a certain level of security or the importance of becoming a corporate leader.

The key to personal management, then, is the process of balancing business and non-business goals and strategies with your needs so that your actions are directed toward achieving those goals.

Some people might argue that following your "gut" reactions or capitalizing on lucky breaks is enough to reach your goals. Perhaps if you don't know where you want to go, you will only recognize it when you get there. A little luck along the way is most welcome, but would you want to risk your future to it?

How to Do Your Personal Planning

If you are an entrepreneur it is essential to know what you want out of life in order to develop your company's activities in that direction. If you are working for someone else, you must know what you want before you can know if your job will give it to you. If you are an enlightened leader of any kind of group you will want to align your people in the direction that the group wants to go—where you want to lead them. If they or you do not have a personal plan that ties into the group's business plan you will find personal tensions pulling the group where the business plan does not want to take it.

The process of planning is more important than the plan itself. It forces you to think through and analyze the goals you want to set and the way that you will achieve them. It requires diligent thought, continuing commitment, self discipline, and help from friends and associates.

Process A collection of activities structured to produce a particular output, usually to satisfy customers.

The first and most important part of the goal-making process is writing it down, step by step. Many people say they have thought through what they want to do and know how they will achieve things. Thinking it through, but not committing it to paper, is only a brush with rational planning. It is food for thought but not an organization of resources, an analysis of the situation, and an examination of your feelings. If you do have a plan in mind you should have a way of monitoring or measuring your progress toward achievement.

Be Able to Define Success You must be able to identify success or you won't have any way of monitoring your progress or knowing if you have achieved your goals.

You don't follow a road map without periodically checking to see if you are still on the path and how much further you have to go. You don't monitor and make adjustments to a plan without having developed a road map that you can check for progress, direction, and timing or scheduling of when you will get there.

Facing the hard print of your commitments helps keep you on schedule, and it also helps you adjust and monitor your plan. But first, you have to develop the plan. Let's look at this step by step in the next lesson.

In this lesson you gained insight into what planning and scheduling is, why personal planning is important, the key to personal management, and how to do it. In the next lesson you learn how to think through your aims and goals and learn a unique method to establish them.

LESSON 2

Setting Aims, Actions, and Schedules for Your Personal Plan

In this lesson you learn how to think through your aims or goals and a unique method to help you establish them.

Creating a Written List of Your Aims

Having a written list of your aims or goals is essential. Before putting your goals on paper, however, try to feel through what your life is like and how you see it. What is its purpose for you? For some people the only purpose in life is to make money. For others the purpose of their lives is to love and be loved; for others, to avoid pain and to seek pleasure. Some dedicate their lives to doing what they most enjoy with those who enjoy the same things.

Goal A long range aim.

Ask yourself what you want out of life. What are the things that make you happy? Consider the following questions:

- What environment have you chosen for yourself—your work environment and your life environment?
- How may others compete with you for your goals? What are their strengths and weaknesses? How capable are they? Are they a real threat? Can the competition be overcome?
- How can you prepare yourself so that your goals can prevail?
- What opportunities do you see as a result of this self-analysis?

Pretty soon a clear picture of what you really want and are good at begins to emerge.

First Things First Without knowing what you want out of life, how will you know what you want out of your business or profession?

The aims or goals that you set may be for your business, profession, other aspects of your life, or a combination of these. Goals should be seriously made and not easily changed. They must be thought through carefully and felt deeply. A "head-to-gut" check, to see if you really want to establish each particular goal, helps keep your goals consistent with how your total being feels about setting out to achieve them. It is also a good idea to talk over the goals with a good friend you trust to be totally honest with you. This reality check needs to be done during the entire process of personal planning in order to help you to be as objective as possible in your decisions.

The following questions may prove to be triggers to help you to establish your goals:

- What would you like to achieve in business or in your profession?
- How much would you like to be earning in a year, five years, and ten years from now?
- What do you want to accomplish to help improve your health?
- What would you like to spend time on other than earning a living?
- Do you want to travel?
- Do you plan to be involved with church, politics, charities, and other social activities?
- Where do you want to live and in what kind of environment?

Make a List If you are not writing it all down, you will not get a clear picture or develop a plan against which you can check your progress.

You probably have goals in areas other than those suggested. Don't underestimate the importance of developing very personal goals and actions or strategies. They provide a clear vision of how to turn your dreams and fantasies into reality. Talk with your friends and family about your dreams, wishes, and desires. This may also help present goals that you may wish to establish.

Strategy A plan used to reach a goal.

Just list your goals or use a goal and strategy format, as shown in Table 2.1, which allows you to put the strategies next to each goal and to work with one goal at a time. As you list each goal, try to list several actions to achieve them or the strategies you will use to accomplish the goal on the form or below the goal on your list. Also, put the time when you expect to complete the action. Later, when you have finished listing your goals and strategies, you can review and refine them.

TABLE 2.1 SAMPLE WORKSHEET FOR LISTING AIMS (GOALS), ACTIONS (STRATEGIES), AND WHEN (SCHEDULE)

AIMS OR GOALS	ACTIONS OR STRATEGIES	WHEN
Make a million dollars	Become an entrepreneur	3 years
	Get a position in my field and learn all I can on the job	6 months
	Finish my formal schooling	2 years
	Build up my capital by saving and by prudent investment	ongoing
	Work toward a partnership in the company I am with and be prepared to go into my own business if it doesn't work out	3 years

AIMS OR GOALS	ACTIONS OR STRATEGIES	WHEN
Spend more time with my loved ones	Take a vacation for at least two weeks every year	6 months
	Go away on a long weekend every three months	3 months
	Be sure to attend 90 percent of my child's Little League games	ongoing
Write a book	First write articles and get published (Note: This can also become a goal.)	1 month
	Get up one hour earlier every day to write	ongoing
	Take a course in writing	6 months
	Talk to writers and find out how they do it	2 weeks

HELP IN DETERMINING YOUR GOALS

If you have trouble knowing what your goals are, there is a proven process that helps develop personal plans. It involves triggering goals by making lists of your traits. The lists should consist of four sets of characteristics:

Likes

Dislikes

Strengths

Weaknesses

List your likes and your dislikes. Also, make a list of your strengths and your weaknesses. Use Table 2.2 as a guide to set up worksheets for your analysis.

Review the Lists When you have completed these lists, review them with a trusted friend, one who you know will be honest with you. Ask that friend to see if your lists, in their view, are a true reflection of you.

In reviewing your strengths and weaknesses with a friend it may be a surprise, for example, to find out that you said you like classical music, but your friend might challenge that. Your friend might ask: "If that's true, why don't you go to any concerts, own any classical records or CDs, or listen to classical music on the radio?" In another instance you might have put "working with people" down as a strength and find yourself challenged by your friend, "If that's so, why do you spend so much time alone, never want to meet new people, and get nervous when working with others?" On the other hand, your observation of yourself might be verified.

After completing the attributes in the four categories, cross-reference the likes with your strengths and your dislikes with your weaknesses. You may be surprised to find that when linking your likes with your strengths you find goals lurking there. Things that you like to do and are good at certainly point the way to positive activities in your life. On the other hand, dislikes and weaknesses should obviously be avoided. Even if you know what your goals are, going through this exercise acts as a reality check on the goals you have already set.

TABLE 2.2 GOAL ANALYSIS AND TRIGGERS FOR SETTING GOALS

STRENGTHS	WEAKNESSES
Analytical	Not people oriented
Express myself well in writing	Not a good public speaker
Problem solving	Too oriented to handling personal problems logically without considering the other person's emotional needs and my own.

LIKES	DISLIKES
Problem solving	Irrational thinking
Writing	Public speaking
Learning about new technical advances	A lot of conversation

Pace Yourself Don't take on too many goals at one time. It will only discourage you if you can't complete all of them.

If possible, have a short list. Allow goals to remain fairly fixed and not easily changed. True, goals are not cast in stone and can and should be changed if appropriate. But consider goal changes carefully. On the other hand, strategies should be flexible, allowing for the vicissitudes in life.

Once you have a personal plan (a basic list of goals and strategies) on a sheet of paper, you can monitor your progress toward achieving what you want out of life. As you achieve each strategy for the goal, check it off the list. When you have achieved a goal successfully, really celebrate. It is not necessary to monitor your goals and strategies daily, but do look at them periodically to see if you are on target. A complete review and any necessary changes should be done annually.

Define Success You must establish what success will be for you so you can monitor your progress toward success.

As you read through this book the personal planning process will become clearer and more meaningful.

In this lesson you have seen examples of how best to go about setting your personal goals and a method to follow for establishing them. In the next lesson you define *plan* and the *planning cycle* and you learn the differences between content and process.

LESSON 3

The Anatomy of a Plan

In this lesson you learn what a plan *and the* planning cycle *are, how to use plans, and the difference between content and process.*

What Is a Plan?

Among the dictionary definitions given for the word *plan* is, *...a method...for...achieving an end b: an often customary method of doing something : PROCEDURE c: a detailed formulation of a program of action : GOAL, AIM (Merriam-Webster's Collegiate Dictionary, 10th ed., s.v. "plan.")*

Plans and planning are more complex than the dictionary definition implies. For example, you could plan a picnic with your romantic partner for a Sunday. The plan would get more complex if you decided the picnic should include that person's parents, and even more complex if you decide the site of the picnic should be 100 miles from home. The more complex the plan, the more complex are the things you have to do to implement the plan.

The actions or strategies to implement the plans for the picnic with your partner are rather simple. You might phone to see if she or he is available on Sunday. If the answer is yes, then the details of where, when, how you would get to the picnic site, and who would bring what might all come into play. But, in reality, it would probably not be considered on a very conscious level. More than likely the details would take care of themselves. Nevertheless, a time would be set to meet, transportation would be agreed upon, and what each of you would bring would be stipulated. The aim or goal—having a picnic—would have been established and the actions or strategies of making it happen would have been agreed upon.

Six Important Questions When constructing a plan, always ask, as Rudyard Kipling suggested, What, Why, When, How, Where, and Who.

If you complicate the picnic by inviting parents and choosing a site many miles away, you add additional issues to the plan. Assuming that all parties agree to the goal of having the picnic, you still need agreement on the strategies. What time will you meet? How will you get there? Who will bring what? Where it will be? Who will pay? And so on. You might even want to develop a contingency plan should the weather be bad. Now the plan is even more complex. It is still a plan of one goal, yet the multitude of strategies and the addition of other players into the plan makes it necessary to do more planning than when only one other person was involved.

Whether you realize it or not you are involved in planning. It might be a simple picnic or something more complex. As a matter of fact, whatever you do usually requires planning, consciously or unconsciously. The more people that get involved in your plan, the more factors you have to consider. As you get involved in your personal and business planning, many goals will require a multitude of strategies in order to develop and implement the plan.

You can begin to see that planning is not a simple process. If, however, you dissect the anatomy of a plan and understand the process of planning, understanding and effectively using plans to achieve the things you want in your life becomes easier.

Anatomy Parts separated for examination.

Content and Process

The process of planning is all important. It makes you think. Sure, you want to have a plan in hand when you have gone through the process, and you will. But keep in mind that the process is never-ending. You must monitor and change the plan as circumstances dictate and as elements of the plan work or fail. It is, however, this process of analyzing, planning, monitoring and re-planning (as seen in Figure 3.1) that is important. The content of the plan is equally important. They are like two people on a seesaw working together to keep a perfect balance.

Presidential Advice Dwight D. Eisenhower said: "Plans are nothing, planning is everything."

Change Is Good Without following this never-ending cycle, you would be locked into plans that might no longer be appropriate and therefore fail.

CONTENT

Content is the hard details of the plan—the goals, strategies, analysis, research, evaluations, budgets, and so on, that you are able to set down on paper and act upon.

PROCESS

Process is the part of planning where you think, conceptualize, and make decisions that lead you to the content. It is also interaction with others to discuss your ideas and to share your feelings and thoughts. It is your mind at work, taking in and analyzing information so that you can put it down on paper.

Remember, the process of planning happens conceptually, not linearly. You should always feel free to move back and forth through the process until your conclusions are satisfactory. The process is also circular, moving from ideas to goals, then to strategies, and often giving rise to other ideas which, in turn, give rise to new or different goals.

Monitoring The means of knowing if your plan is moving in the envisioned direction.

Measuring Quantifying the monitoring, usually against standards that you have set to be achieved.

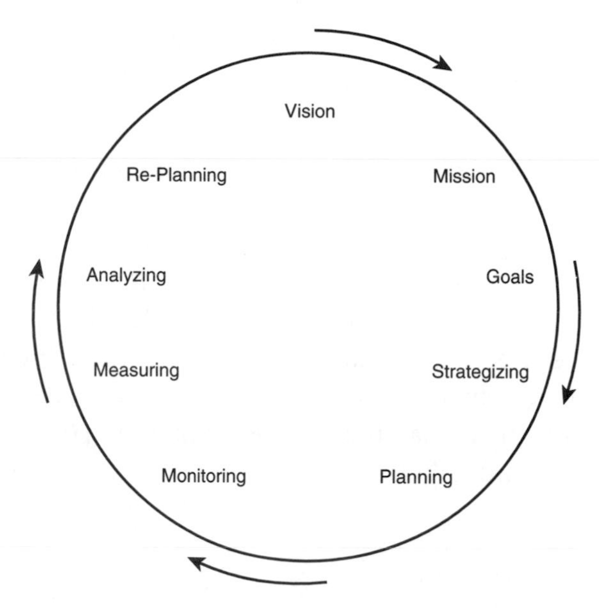

Figure 3.1 This never-ending cycle is a path to achieving goals.

What Are Plans Used For?

Recently I was discussing planning with father and son clients. I tried to emphasize the importance of planning to the son and to explain the process when the father said, "I have never planned in my life." I was startled, for this remark came from a rather successful businessman. When I asked, "Why do you say that?" his reply was, "Well, events just carried me from one job to another and then into my own business."

I think he truly believed he never did any planning. When I pressed him further, it turned out that, "Of course I planned, but the best things that happened to me were just luck." I asked, "Then you make no plans for operating your business and you have no plans to pass on the business to your son?" He said, "Oh, no! You have to plan for your business and, of course, I have personal plans for how and when I want to turn over my business to my son."

We went on and on and finally decided that it was all a matter of semantics. Planning was being done during the early stages of his life. In his words, he was "just taking advantage of breaks that developed by placing myself at the right place at the right time." But he actually planned it. He made mental plans and strategies without knowing it. When he thought back, he realized that he did have a road he wanted to travel and he knew how he wanted to travel it. He did have personal plans, but he had separated the idea of planning out of his personal life and only thought of it in relation to business.

Don't Keep Your Plans a Secret You must share your plans with those whom you expect to help you implement them.

USE PLANS FOR A VARIETY OF PURPOSES

- Plans help you analyze where you are and can point the way to where you want to be.
- Plans help you determine the business you might want to go into and the best way to enter and conduct that business.
- Plans help you to operate your present business and can be used to raise money for your enterprise from investors, banks, venture capitalists, the public, and other sources.

- Plans also tell your associates and employees where you are heading and how you expect to get there.
- Planning projects your expectations and the direction you are taking.
- Sharing portions of your plan with customers, suppliers, and others in the trade sets the tone for your company in the marketplace.
- Plans are also a means to monitor performance, whether personally or professionally.

In this lesson you learned what a plan is, the planning cycle, the use of plans, and the difference between content and process. The next lesson discusses a business's three-year rolling plan, the seven basic elements of planning, ten searching questions to ask in planning, and assumptions to make in planning.

The Eight Elements of Planning

In this lesson you learn about the three-year business rolling plan, the eight basic elements of planning, ten searching questions to ask in planning, and assumptions to make in planning.

Why Start with a Three-Year Rolling Plan?

Unless you are planning to build a power plant, railroad, chemical plant, or any kind of project that will take many years to implement, it is best to plan for short horizons. Even five-year planning, the former mainstay of most business organizations, is too long for today's fast track. Changes in the marketplace, the economy, and the world are happening so fast it is impossible to plan too far in advance. At one time you could take five years to develop and bring out a new product or start up a new business and achieve profitability. Today, eighteen months is about how long it takes to bring out a new product and you would try to develop profits in the first year of a new business in order to make your way through today's tough competition.

Behavioral scientists have found that productivity in picking beans, for example, increased considerably when colored string was placed across the field. With the string, pickers had a visual point by which to measure their progress instead of gazing down a seemingly endless row. You too will find that short-term goals are a motivator and tend to prevent you or your associates from becoming discouraged when attempting to accomplish what you have all set out to do.

Therefore, I would strongly suggest that you plan for short segments and that the segments be developed into three-year rolling plans. I like rolling plans rather than fixed ones because you change the last or third year of the plan as you make adjustments and generally leave the first two years of the plan intact (see Table 4.1). The three-year rolling plan is therefore being updated yearly to accommodate the changes taking place within the environment you are operating in, yet you maintain your goals and have clear plans for at least a two-year period.

Three-Year Rolling Plan A process by which you plan for three years and at the end of the first year you again plan the third year leaving the first and second years intact. In other words, each year you roll over the first two years and plan the third.

TABLE 4.1 PLANNING STRUCTURE FOR THE THREE-YEAR ROLLING PLAN

YEARS	1	2	3	4	5
	Plan All Three				
First Year	1	2	3		
				Plan	
Second Year	Done	1	2	3	
					Plan
Third Year		Done	1	2	3

Plans need to be:

- Flexible
- Monitored
- Frequently analyzed

Changes should not be made lightly, but made as required. Even if you are operating on the basis of a three-year rolling plan, sometimes you cannot wait for changes to be made in the third year. You have to break into the cycle and make immediate changes. Of course this should be done only with very careful thought and only for absolutely necessary reasons.

You can also use a fixed one-year, two-year, or three-year plan. In some situations, as I previously indicated, even a five-year or longer plan may be required. The key is this: *The form of the plan should follow the function needed.* Only you can determine what length and type of plan your situation calls for.

Watch the Skies Monitor your market and know when changes are taking place that will affect your plan. If you do, you'll know when to break into the planning cycle and re-plan.

EIGHT ELEMENTS OF PLANNING

Overall planning for your business is a must, but you may also need more specific plans for the various functions or disciplines of your business, such as marketing, finance, production, and so on. Sometimes the planning is only for a trade show, the installation of new equipment, or a move to larger quarters. Some plans fit inside the bigger or overall plans. The elements of planning, however, apply to whatever planning you are doing.

Mind Your Business If you can define what business you are in, it will help you in developing the elements of your plan.

The basic elements of planning are:

- **Vision** The leader must set forth and communicate a clear concept of what defines the business, the company's philosophy, creed, purpose, beliefs, business principles, and, therefore, what is visualized. This vision must be shared by all who are planning to turn it into reality.
- **Mission** The organization's mission is second only to developing a shared vision. A mission statement should define the business that the company is in, as well as its major goals, characteristics, and guiding philosophies. It also tells everyone what the company has set forth to accomplish.
- **Goals** Your long-term aims. Whether personal or in business, goals are the destinations you want to reach.
- **Strategies** The way you will accomplish your aims or goals. Strategies are how you are going to arrive at the destinations you have set forth in your goals.
- **Monitoring** The means of knowing if your plan is moving in the envisioned direction. Just as you follow a map to reach a certain town and constantly check the road signs and your position on the map

to see if you are still on the right road, so you must monitor your plan to see if it is being achieved.

- **Measuring** Quantifying the monitoring, usually against standards that you have set to be achieved. On a trip you would automatically measure how many more miles to go, determine if you are where you expected to be at the time you planned, if it looks like you will arrive at the prescribed place on time, if you will have enough money to complete the trip, and so on.
- **Analysis** Reviewing and studying all factors so that you can adjust your plan if necessary. As data comes in, it should tell you where you are and how well you are doing in relation to the plan. The information, however, must be reviewed and an assessment made as to whether the strategies are working or if you need to change destinations (goals).
- **Re-planning** Setting or reconfirming your vision, mission, goals, and strategies.

Write It Down "The finest memory is not so firm as faded ink," *Lao-Tse*.

TEN QUESTIONS TO ASK DURING THE PLANNING PROCESS

The planning process requires a great deal of thought and analysis. Following is a list of 10 searching questions that must be continually asked during this process.

1. Where are we now?
2. Where do we want to go?
3. How do we get there?
4. When do we want to arrive?
5. Who will get us there?
6. What will it cost?
7. How do we measure results?
8. Who will help accomplish the plan?
9. When will each strategy and goal be completed?
10. What are the expected results?

LOOKING AT THE PROCESS GRAPHICALLY

Internal Environment The circumstances, objectives, and conditions that surround you inside your company.

External Environment The circumstances, objectives, and conditions of the markets within which you will be competing.

The chart in Figure 4.1 shows the basic steps in the planning process. It also indicates that you must examine the internal environment and external environment to be sure that you have the necessary resources and the correct picture of the marketplace. You must do this examination to be sure that the resources you have are adequate to accomplish the goals and strategies that you are developing. It is also necessary to research and study the market to determine whether the goals and strategies you are setting for yourself or your company are realistic in the marketplace.

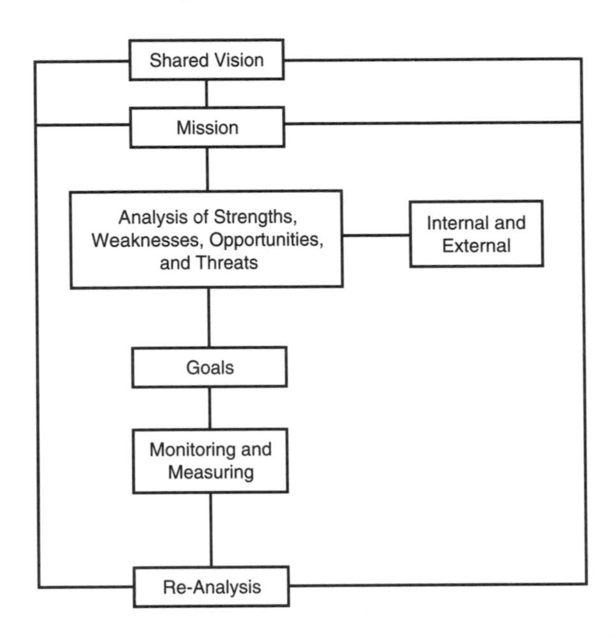

Figure 4.1 The process incorporates internal and external forces.

PLANNING OFTEN BEGINS WITH ASSUMPTIONS

Planning deals with the future. To deal with the unknown we often have historical data that we can analyze. This helps, but it cannot always predict future events. For that reason assumptions must be made. Decisions are based on these assumptions.

An analysis of the company's *Strengths, Weaknesses, Opportunities, and Threats* (SWOT) will lead to making reasonable assumptions. The SWOT analysis is discussed in Lesson 10.

Reality Check If assumptions are not as realistic as humanly possible, they may lead to a plan with false premises. That is why a SWOT Analysis is vital.

Estimates or assumptions of the future should be made for such factors as:

- Market outlook
- Price trends
- Economic developments, both domestic and global
- Fiscal actions
- Capital available
- Government regulations, restrictions, and actions
- Tax rates
- Population growth
- Business cycles
- Competition

The planning process is essential and plans are vital in your personal, professional, or business life. You can consciously plan and thereby take your destiny into your own hands or you can rely on your unconscious to direct your life. If you cannot bring your unconscious thoughts to the surface to examine them in the light of logic, they may remain buried within you as unrealized dreams.

Writing down your plan forces you to clearly think through what you are doing. It is also essential so that you can monitor and measure results. Without a written plan, your mind can play tricks on you. You can forget your goals and strategies, or worse, distort them. There is nothing in this book that I more strongly recommend than to write out the planning process and the plan.

In this lesson you learned about the three-year business rolling plan, the eight basic elements of planning, ten searching questions to ask in planning, and assumptions to make in planning. In the next lesson you learn what a shared vision is and why you need one for your stakeholders; you also see several examples of vision statements.

LESSON 5

VISIONING

In this lesson you learn what a shared vision is and why you need one for your stakeholders. This lesson also provides several examples of vision statements.

VISUALIZING WHAT YOU WANT TO CREATE

The most important thing to have before you can do any planning is a vision. How can you plan without knowing what you envision for yourself, your department, your business unit, your company, your organization, or whatever you are planning for? It would be like starting an automobile trip without having first envisioned your destination, purpose of the trip, and what you expect to accomplish.

There is the practical aspect, too. In their study of successful companies, Collins and Porras found that those companies performed eight times better than companies that were not visionary and did not have a shared vision statement. Visionary companies also performed 55 times better than the overall stock market. True, some giant companies do not subscribe to having a vision, but from my observations they do not optimize their results.

Think about it! If you don't have a clear picture of what you want to create and how you want your organization to be, how will you marshal your resources toward that end?

WHAT IS A VISION?

Vision A way of seeing or conceiving what you or your organization wants to create or achieve.

Vision statements should be developed for your organization and may also be developed for your department or business unit, a charity, or whatever group you are planning for. A personal vision might be to write a practical, easy-to-understand book on planning. It is, in fact, my vision for this book. You might have a personal vision of wealth or to create a business. Whatever you envision is what you will be reaching for in your planning.

The following examples of vision statements show some of the different kinds of statements used to reflect an organization's vision.

Three-Sided Compass The three primary indicators of the direction in which you or your organization will move are the vision, the mission, and the goals.

American Marketing Association (AMA)—"The American Marketing Association is dedicated to being the ultimate source of knowledge and training for understanding, meeting, and exceeding customer expectations through the application of marketing principles."

Entergy Corporation—"Winning through innovative and profitable actions—exceeding customer expectations everywhere we serve."

GTE—"We will be an international leader in telecommunications."

Institute Of Management Consultants (IMC)—"To advance the practice of management consulting as an art and science; to develop standards for admissions to the Institute of Management Consultants; to promote and organize a program of research, publications, seminars, conferences, education, and training in the field of management consulting; to take all the necessary steps to help individual management consultants achieve professional status; to promote working relationships with related professional groups."

New York State Electric & Gas Corporation (NYSEG)—"Put energy into action, providing ever better quality and value to those we serve. We seek to set the standard for excellence, leadership and integrity in the utility industry."

Personal Vision—"Write a practical, easy to understand book on planning."

Weyerhaeuser Company, Inc.—"The best Forest Products Company in the World."

SHARING A VISION IS IMPERATIVE

In order to have a vision that is translated into action it must be shared. If it is a personal vision, it should be shared with your loved ones and friends. If it is a vision for your organization, it must be shared with all the stakeholders. People cannot help you to achieve your vision unless they know what it is and become as committed to it as you are. You will be surprised where help and counsel come from when you share your vision with others.

Divided We Fall If your vision is not shared with all those that have a stake in your business, you will have trouble moving toward that vision.

Stakeholders Those that have a vested interest in what the organization does.

An organizational vision cannot be something that is merely published and passed out to everyone. It cannot be imposed or handed down as a directive from on high. It must be lived by the leaders and accepted by all if it is to become a vision that has everyone working toward the same ends. To gain that acceptance, however, may not be so easy. Top-down or one-shot visions are usually not shared. They are just something that people have been handed. It is what they have been instructed to do.

Shared vision, on the other hand, is when all the people are committed to the vision and therefore committed to making it happen. It usually dove-tails with the individual's vision. When that happens, people generally feel free to make things happen, to be creative, take initiative, and espouse the vision—not just follow orders. Of course to fulfill the vision, the company culture must foster creativity and allow people to be responsible and creative in taking action.

To have a shared vision, consider the following things:

1. The company culture must foster individual thinking and actions and provide fertile ground for commitment, not just compliance.
2. The people must be part of creating the vision.
3. The people can't be sold on the vision; they must convince themselves to adapt.
4. The leaders must believe in the vision and live it.
5. The vision should be a simple, honest statement that describes the purpose of the organization.
6. The vision should give a picture of the future being sought.
7. It should be consistent with the core values of the people in the organization.
8. The shared vision should be a launching platform for the company's mission.

Walk the Walk An organization's vision must be lived by the leaders of that organization. It can't just be talked about—it has to be practiced.

Too often, the actions ofthe "keepers of the vision" are different from and conflict with what would be expected to sustain the vision. Often only top management is behind the vision, knows what it is, or does not share it with everyone. On the other hand, everyone may know what is written in the vision statement but they may interpret and perceive it differently, or just not accept it at all. *That is why it is essential that the vision be understood, shared, accepted, and lived by everyone responsible for making it a reality.* (See Figure 5.1.)

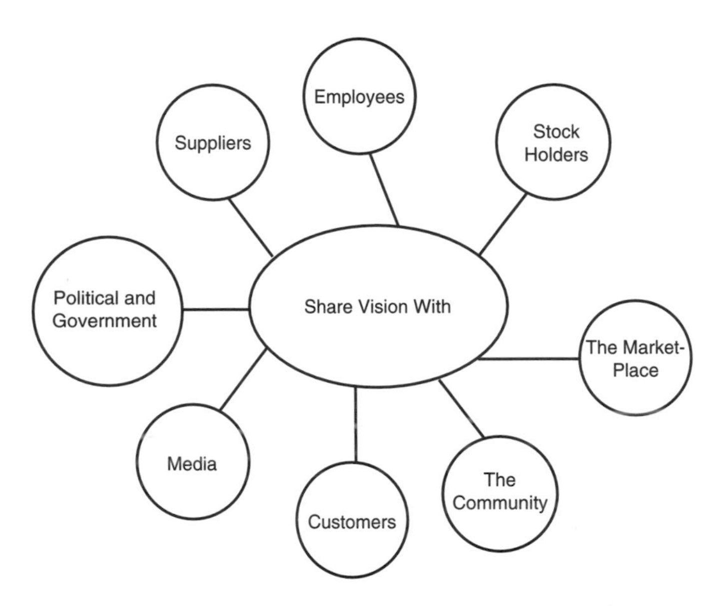

Figure 5.1 **The stakeholder's shared vision reaches far outside the company walls.**

Figure 5.1 indicates stakeholders—groups of people with whom you should consider sharing your vision. They all impact on the success of the company and should understand what your company is trying to create. If suppliers know what you are trying to achieve, not just what you want to buy from them, they may well be able to contribute ideas and actions to help you fulfill your vision. Customers, too, feel more like your partners and not just someone being sold something if they understand where your company is headed. Your stockholders and others can be part of what you are trying to achieve if they are aware of your vision.

In this lesson you learned what a shared vision is and why you need one for your stakeholders. You also saw examples of vision statements. In the next lesson you learn what a mission statement is, why it is important, what it can do for you, what it should cover, and examples of effective mission statements.

Developing a Mission

In this lesson you learn what a mission statement is, why it is important, what it can do for you, and what it should cover.

What Is a Mission?

A mission lets you, in your personal life, and everyone, in an organization, know who you are and what you want to achieve. It also usually contains your main goals.

Mission A sending forth of yourself or the people in an organization to take actions that will accomplish the vision.

What Is a Mission Statement?

Some companies have different names for their vision or mission statements, such as a Corporate Values, Corporate Philosophy, Goals, and so on. Others freely interchange one for the other. Don't be rigid. Definitions are not important; they are only guides. Content is what is important. What is essential is that whatever they are called, they should be carefully developed and diligently shared.

The Mission Is the Foundation As the last lesson noted, the three primary indicators of the direction in which you or your organization will move are the *vision*, the *mission*, and the *goals*. The mission, however, is the overall reason an organization exists.

The organizational mission must answer the big question, "What is our business, or what business are we in?" In personal planning, the big question to be answered is, "What is my life's business?" In either case, the answer should define the reason for being.

Know Your Purpose If you can't answer the question "Why do we exist?" you can't develop a plan that can feed what you need in order to continue to exist.

The mission statement is also a practical document that states what you are and what you have set out to do. The mission statement should not, however, set forth concrete actions, but instead, define the abstract concepts to be achieved.

A mission statement carries out the following tasks:

- Indicates how resources will be allocated.
- Sets the tone of the organization.

- Rallies people to a common purpose.
- Helps establish the desired culture within which the organization will operate.
- Lets the world know where you are headed.
- Provides motivation.
- Gives direction.
- Establishes a philosophy.
- Reconciles the differences of stakeholders. Stakeholders are those who have a stake in what happens to the organization, such as customers, vendors, employees, and so on.
- Evokes feelings of success.
- Generally, indicates that the organization warrants support.

According to a survey, Fortune 500 Companies with comprehensive mission statements were more profitable than companies with sparse ones. Anecdotal evidence also indicates that the more people who know and understand the mission, the more likely it is to be achieved.

WHAT SHOULD A MISSION STATEMENT COVER?

Here are the basics for writing a mission statement. You might find other elements that you want to include:

- The type of products or services that you plan to offer. In your personal planning, it is what you have to offer.

- Your intended customers and markets. In personal planning, it is to whom you will offer what you have.
- The values of the organization or yourself.
- The direction to be taken.
- Technologies and capabilities.
- The general mention of goals.
- The philosophy of the organization or of yourself.
- The company's view of itself and, in personal planning, your view of yourself.
- How the organization will relate to its employees and how you will relate to those who employ you.
- The public image.

DETERMINING CORE

ValuesPeter M. Senge, in his acclaimed book The Fifth Discipline, said that core values answer the question "How do we want to act, consistent with our mission, along the path toward achieving our vision?"

Core Values The central worth or importance that an organization holds in highest esteem.

Core values deal with such things as how the organization will act in relation to honesty, integrity, openness, loyalty, and in general, how you will treat the people you do business with—including employees. In planning, you have to know where you're going, but you also have to know who and what you are. The core values define this for you and your organization.

Practice What You Preach Consistent application of core values defines your organization for all who deal with it.

Here are some well-known organizations' published mission statements to guide you in writing your own mission statement:

American Marketing Association (AMA)—"The American Marketing Association is an international, professional society of individual members with an interest in the practice, study, and teaching of marketing. Our principal rules are:

> First, to urge and assist the personal and professional development of our members, and
>
> Second, to advance the science and ethical practice of the marketing discipline."

Arthritis Foundation—"Support research to find the cure for and prevention of arthritis and to improve the quality of life for those affected by arthritis."

AT&T—"We are dedicated to being the world's best at bringing people together—giving them easy access to each other and to the information and services they want and need anytime, anywhere."

Caterpillar, Inc.—"Provide differentiated products and services of recognized superior value to discriminating customers worldwide.

Pursue businesses which we can be a leader, based on one or more of our strengths.

Build and maintain a productive work environment in which high levels of personal satisfaction can be achieved while conforming to our code of worldwide business conduct and operating principals.

Achieve growth and above-average returns for stockholders, resulting from both management of ongoing businesses and a studied awareness and development of new opportunities."

GTE—"To fulfill this vision, we remain dedicated to achieving three key objectives:

To be recognized by the media and the public as one of the world's great companies in performance and management effectiveness;

To be acknowledged as a world leader in all our businesses—by providing products and services that meet customer expectations in terms of quality and cost; and,

To maximize shareholders' long-term total return, as measured by share-price appreciation and dividends.

Furthermore, we set an ambitious goal: to increase return on equity to 20%."

Institute of Management Consultants (IMC)—"Establish professional and ethical standards for management consultants.

Admit into membership, certify, professionals who meet IMC's established standards.

Provide continuing education and information relevant to the development of management consultants.

Increase public awareness of the profession of management consulting."

3M Statement of Mission or Corporate Values—"We are committed to:

Satisfying our *customers* with superior quality and value,

Providing *investors* with an attractive return through sustained, high-quality growth,

Respecting our social and physical environment,

Being a company that *employees* are proud to be a part of."

March to the Same Drummer If you don't have a shared mission, not everyone in your organization will go forth to achieve the same thing.

The mission statement is a product of shared visions, but it will and should change as your goals and strategies are established. It is a living document to be updated as the internal and external environments evolve within which you or the organization operates; it changes as you re-analyze and update your plan.

In this lesson you learned what a mission statement is, why it is important, what it can do for you, and what it should cover. You also saw examples of a variety of corporate and organizational mission statements. In the next lesson you learn the difference between goals, objectives, tactics, and strategy. You also learn how a small company set its goals and the homework they had to do, as well as how to integrate your goals with your mission.

LESSON 7

Setting Goals or Aims

In this lesson you learn the difference between goals, objectives, tactics, and strategy; how a small company sets its goals; the homework that company had to do; how to integrate your goals with your mission; and what you should set goals for.

What Are Goals?

Some people use the term *objectives* interchangeably with goals. For me, however, there is a difference. An objective is a short-range aim, such as a seasonal advertising plan. It has a shorter horizon than a goal but a longer horizon than a tactic. A tactic is a device for accomplishing an immediate specific end, such as how to approach a customer to make a sale now.

Goals The long-range aims or end-points that you want to reach.

DEFINITIONS ARE NOT IMPORTANT

Definitions, however, are not important as long as you and those who will be affected by them are clear about what you mean when you say a certain term. Call your end-aims what you will. Just know that unless you do set clear end-aims, you and your associates will not know what you are trying to achieve.

Summarizing the definitions, they are:

- **Goal** Long-range aim
- **Objective** Short-range aim
- **Tactic** A device for accomplishing an immediate end
- **Strategy** How to get to the end-aim

Don't Sacrifice Quality Speed in planning and execution is important, but not at the expense of quality or execution.

With horizons accelerated in all phases of organizational activity, it is impossible to designate how many years you should plan for the completion of your long-term aims or to reach the end-points of your goals. An end-point can be one, two, three, five, or even fifteen years. It depends on what you are planning. If your goal is engineering and building a power plant, it could take ten years or more. If your goal or long-term aim is to write a book, it might have a two-year end-point. To bring a new product to market might have an eighteen-month end-point.

Setting Goals for a Small Company

About eight years ago, when I was still a partner in a sales agency, we faced a rapidly changing and deteriorating market. We had done planning but not strategic planning. Our plans were projections based on history and not on an analysis of our internal resources and the external conditions of the market. Faced with a dearth of customers and declining revenues, we decided to do a strategic plan.

Because I had experience in strategic planning and was no longer involved in the day-to-day activities of that business, I was asked to direct and facilitate the process. We also agreed that a one-day meeting of everyone in the company—about twelve people—was essential in order to get their input. An additional benefit was to have those involved in implementing the plan be part of its development.

Assigning Individual Homework

Prior to our meeting, everyone was asked to prepare a one-page or shorter list of their views for each of the following:

1. Their vision of the company as they look ahead.
2. Their perception of the company's mission.
3. The company goals as they see them.
4. Their personal goals in relation to the company's goals.
5. In their eyes, a list of the company's strengths, weaknesses, opportunities, and threats (known as a SWOT analysis).

6. The company's critical issues.
7. The business they think we are now in and what it should be in the future.
8. Suggestions on actions the company should take.
9. A list of their core competencies (what the company is best at and what skills can benefit customers).
10. Their estimation of their best skills in the eyes of their customers.
11. Their impressions of what the company's core competencies should be in three to five years.
12. Suggestions on actions the company should take.

I reviewed all the submissions and then interviewed each person to obtain clarity and amplification on their reports. I promised and gave everyone complete confidentiality.

We then held our full-day meeting. A compilation of all the written reports and personal interviews were reported to the group. No information was attributed to any one individual. After the summary report was given, we discussed it and then listed any and all comments, thoughts, and ideas it evoked. From that list we could isolate the critical issues and define the business we were in. Then the leader and president of the company stated his vision. Everyone was asked to give their vision for the company as well. Again it was discussed and notes were taken. Later a vision was articulated and shared with everyone.

INTEGRATING GOALS WITH THE MISSION

Next we worked on the mission. What did people think they had to go forth and do? We again kept notes, and at a later time, we formalized a mission statement.

At this point in the process, we wanted everyone's ideas freely stated and summarized into goals. No discussion, criticism, or comment was permitted during this phase. After we had all the goals, no matter how wild, we discussed them. We then eliminated some and prioritized what remained. Unanimity was essential before a goal was actually adopted and strategies developed.

This story cannot nearly convey all the work that was involved nor the details of the process used. It was, however, one way that a small company went about establishing its goals. I believe it was the establishment of these goals that allowed the company to change and accommodate the new needs of the market. Everyone in the company was fully behind the effort because they were all part of the process. It worked! The company is now very successful and profitably serving its principals and customers.

Keep in mind that different circumstances dictate when and how you or your organization should set or reset goals.

Be Able to Gauge Success If you don't have a way of measuring your goals you won't know if you are achieving them.

KNOWING IF YOU'RE ACHIEVING YOUR GOALS

The only way you know if you are achieving your goals is to have very clear standards or targets by which to measure the relative success of each goal. The following list represents just a few of the areas for which you will want to establish standards or targets:

Sales

Profits

Cash flow

Return on investment

Growth rate

Market position

Market share

Productivity

New product development or innovation

and more, which the next lesson addresses.

It is up to you, as you set each goal, to establish what success will be. The next lesson offers a form, Figure 8.1, to help you establish your goals. You will notice that the form asks "How To Measure" the goal. That is where you will set the standard by which you measure success.

Standard The rule that management establishes to measure the results of goal-oriented activities.

WHO OR WHAT NEEDS GOALS?

Goals should be set for all of the following people and entities:

- Yourself
- The organization
- Business units
- Divisions
- Functional areas
- Individual projects

You Might Have to Set Goals by Yourself If your organization does not set goals for you or your area you should set them yourself.

Mission statements set the broad goals for an organization. You need specific goals, however, for your specific area of work. Without them there can be no clear direction to your efforts or the efforts of those involved with you. That is why if the organization sets no goals beyond the organizational level, you must become your own strategic planner.

In this lesson you learned the difference between goals, objectives, tactics, and strategy; how a small company set its goals; the homework they had to do; how to integrate your goals with your mission; and what you should set goals for. In the next lesson you learn: what helps you in setting goals, how to use a special worksheet to set your goals and strategies, and examples of goals derived from a mission statement.

Aids in Setting Goals

In this lesson you learn what helps you in setting goals, how to use a special worksheet to set your goals and strategies, and examples of goals derived from a mission statement.

There Is No Best Way to Set Goals

Some organizations set autocratic goals; top management just hands them down. Others develop goals from the bottom up. They ask people to provide a list of goals, but usually top management makes the judgment of which goals are adopted and excluded. Some set only corporate goals and leave the operational goals to be set by those who manage. If the organization has a central, strategic, planning group, I suggest that it function as a resource provider, facilitator, and orchestrator, but not as the central planner who just hands down a plan.

Goals Should Be Set by Those Who Will Ultimately Achieve Them Whatever method your organization uses to set goals, I strongly recommend that you work toward having those who will implement the goals develop them.

The form illustrated in Figure 8.1 is designed to help you develop your goals. Use one form for each goal. The goal is stated at the top of the form. Rank is left blank at first. Once you have assembled all the goals, rank them in order of their importance. Then list strategies along with who is responsible, the date of completion, some idea of what it will cost, what benefit or return you expect the strategy will bring, how you will measure the results you are getting, and then a rank for the strategies. In the development of the form we try to force the user to go through the process of addressing the following issues:

- **What**—Goal
- **How**—Strategy
- **Who**—People who will do it
- **When**—Time frame
- **Investment**—What it will cost
- **Why**—The expected return
- **Measure**—To know if you are successful

Content Matters The type of form you use to develop your goals and strategies, however, is not important as long as you get the complete information down.

Goal: ____________________

Rank: ____________________

STRATEGY	PERSON(S) RESPONSIBLE	DATE TO BE COMPLETED	WHAT IT WILL COST	EXPECTED RETURN	HOW TO MEASURE	RANK

Figure 8.1 Form for developing goals and strategies.

Some people like to use computer-guided programs; others prefer listing goals and working in a linear fashion. A linear approach to goal setting, however, does not allow you to integrate all factors. That is why I prefer to work in a more conceptual fashion. Get the concepts down, examine the data, analyze, reevaluate, and in general work back and forth on goals and strategies. When you try to develop strategies, you often find the goals are unrealistic. You also find that goals can sometimes become strategies and strategies goals.

Concepts Abstract ideas that are generalized from particular instance.

Because of the information you learn as you go through the goal-setting process, I believe it is best to freely move back and forth and around all factors in order to arrive at the best possible and most realistic goals.

Following is a good example of goals that are derived from a mission (see Lesson 4)—the mission statement developed by 3M:

3M Corporate Values (Mission Statement)

"Satisfying our customers with superior quality & value—

Our goals are:

> Providing the highest quality products and services consistent with our customers' requirements and preferences.
>
> Making every aspect of every transaction a satisfying experience for our customers.
>
> Finding innovative ways to make life easier and better for our customers.

Providing investors an attractive return through sustained, high-quality growth—

Our goals are:

> Growth in earnings per share averaging 10 percent a year or better,
>
> A return on capital employed of 27 percent or better,
>
> A return on stockholders' equity of between 20 and 25 percent,
>
> At least 30 percent of our sales each year from products new in the last four years.

Respecting our social and physical environment—

Our goals are:

> Complying with all laws and meeting or exceeding regulations,
>
> Keeping customers, employees, investors and the public informed about our operations,
>
> Developing products and process that have a minimal impact on the environment,
>
> Staying attuned to the changing needs and preferences of our customers, employees and society,
>
> Uncompromising honesty and integrity in every aspect of our operations.

Being a company that our employees are proud to be part of—

Our goals are:

> Respecting the dignity and worth of individuals,
>
> Encouraging individual initiative and innovation in an atmosphere characterized by flexibility, cooperation and trust,

> Challenging individual capabilities,
>
> Valuing human diversity and providing equal opportunity for development."

Notice how 3M has covered their stakeholders. They spell out how they will relate to their employees, society, stockholders, and customers. They quantify the results they are targeting. Most importantly, the company shares them with all stakeholders and, if you were to talk to most 3M employees, you would find that they clearly understand and accept the company goals as if they were their own.

MEASURING RESULTS

Know How to Define Success If you don't know what will be considered success, it will be difficult to measure your journey toward it.

When we asked the CEO of one client, "What will you consider success for the assignment you just gave us?", he told us that if we just installed the process we were engaged to develop, he would consider it a success. When we spoke to the presidents of the operating companies, however, they had very different criteria. Each of them had specific, quantifiable results in mind which they would use to measure whether the process was in place and working properly. They wanted agreement that the measuring tool would be a certain amount of dollars generated by the process in relation to the dollars invested. Until we sorted out that a specific dollar return was expected, in addition to a process being in place, we had no solid means of measuring results. In goal setting, as in project development, it is wise to clearly understand the specific definition of success for each goal.

Once the goals have been established and strategies developed, they must be constantly monitored and measured to determine if you are on course toward success.

In addition to quantitative measures such as sales figures, return on investment, return on equity, profits, market share, earnings, and so on, you should measure your progress by asking:

- Are you meeting the time targets?
- Are you on budget?
- Are projected results happening as planned?
- Are attitudes within the organization still enthusiastic toward the goal?
- Is the goal still consistent with the organizational vision and mission?
- How close are you to achieving the goal?
- After re-reviewing the expected return, can you still anticipate the same or a better return for your investment?
- How do actual results compare to expected results?

Monitoring key factors should be ongoing. Measuring, however, must be done when an alert is triggered and at regular intervals. The time intervals for measuring are generally determined by the nature of the goal.

Seek Others' Opinions Measuring should be done by individuals who are objective. It is usually wise to have it done by more than one person and by people from various disciplines.

In this lesson you learned what will help you in setting goals, how to use a special worksheet to set your goals and strategies, and examples of goals derived from a mission statement. In the next lesson you learn how to set strategies in order to achieve your goals, the characteristics of a strategic decision, circular planning, and why planning never ends.

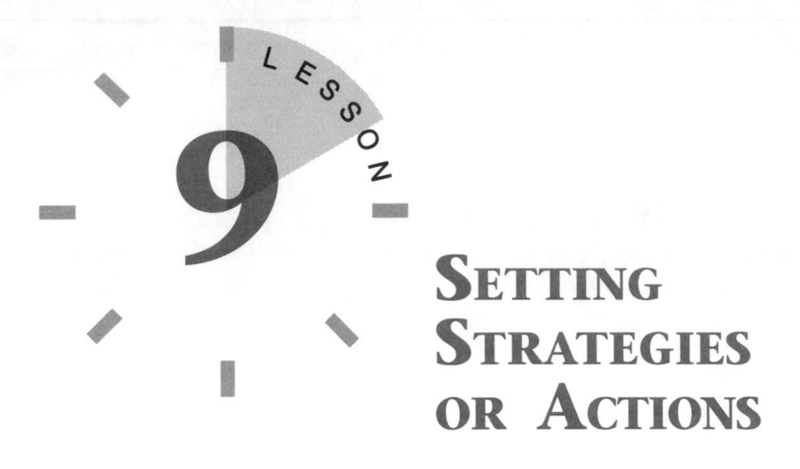

Setting Strategies or Actions

In this lesson you learn how to set strategies in order to achieve your goals, the characteristics of a strategic decision, circular planning, and why planning never ends.

Strategies—Where Planning Meets the Road

The strategies or actions you decide on are the way you plan to achieve your end-aims or goals. You might say it is how you get done what you want to achieve.

Strategy How to get to the end-aim.

Strategies, therefore, need to be developed for every goal and objective you plan to implement. *As a matter of fact, whatever you do in order to achieve anything—consciously or unconsciously—you use strategies.* For example, when you drive to work, you know your goal is to arrive by a given time. Your strategy is probably to take a certain route—one you may drive every day. If, however, you hear on the radio that there's a traffic jam on your regular route, you will probably figure out an alternate route in order to achieve your goal to get to work on time. You have gone from an unconscious strategy to a conscious one, so remember:

- To develop a successful plan, all aspects of the process must be brought in to full consciousness.
- You should plan with maximum information about the environment you will operate within.
- You must have a thorough understanding of the resources available in order to accomplish your goals, objectives, or aims.

Strategies are not just for major goals. They're needed for all aspects and at every level that actions are required. You also need them for every type of planning, such as personal planning, organizations, companies, business units, divisions, departments, functional areas, competition, products, services, investments, and so forth.

Later in the book we review the various areas within an organization that require strategies in order to implement goals.

Think of the Results When thinking of developing strategies think about the impact they will have on your organization.

CHARACTERISTICS OF A STRATEGIC DECISION

Consider the following facts about strategies:

- They tend to change the purpose or direction of the organization.
- More often than not they involve unusual risk in the event of failure.
- Unusual benefits can be gained in the event of success.
- They usually require a commitment for a long period of time.
- Backing and support is generally required at the highest level of responsibility for your activities.
- A series of "go/no-go" decisions is often required.

GOALS AND STRATEGIES SOMETIMES TRADE PLACES

In the planning process, goals give rise to strategies and strategies sometimes become goals of their own. An example: If you have set a goal to start your own business, one of your strategies might be to work for someone in that same business area to learn all that you can about the business before you open your own.

The strategy of working for someone can become its own goal, which requires its own set of strategies. To get a job in your chosen field you might set some of these strategies: Prepare a resume, contact headhunters, get advice from people within the chosen field, contact the editors or publishers of all the trade media in that field, attend the key trade shows, and so on.

There are times when a goal becomes a strategy. For example, to develop a training program may be a goal. It may also become a strategy for improving the effectiveness of the people in your organization.

Don't Fear Changes You have to be alert to when a goal becomes a strategy and when a strategy becomes a goal. Don't be afraid if a goal is also a strategy.

The form in Lesson 8 (Figure 8.1) helps you to sort this out. Be diligent in plotting each goal on a separate form, then list your strategies for accomplishing these goals, along with the time frame, costs, and so on. You will readily see where some things switch from goal to strategy or vice versa. Often this switch takes place in a different time period from the initial planning period. Don't be concerned with it. Take it into account, but persist in pursuing the goals needed to obtain your vision and mission.

PLANNING IS NOT LINEAR

Remember, planning is not necessarily sequential or linear, but rather circular and conceptual. Although logical steps must be taken in planning, the process itself (as represented in the circular diagram shown in Figure 3.1 of Lesson 3) indicates that you can break into the circle at any time to re-evaluate, re-analyze, re-plan, and so forth.

In other cultures, such as the Far East and Middle East, people think much more conceptually than we do in the Western world. We tend to think very sequentially and logically. We make lists and go from point to point. Conceptual thinkers, on the other hand, tend to look at the overall picture and think first in terms of concepts. They have less trouble than we do of seeing planning in a circular fashion. We go through one stage at a time and, when all stages are completed, think we are through planning. The conceptual approach is more circular or, better still, like a spiral. You can go back to any part and revisit it again while making progress toward the actions you will take.

Revision Is Good Good planning always connects all the steps in the planning process, and a good planner never has qualms about going back to a previous step when and if necessary.

THE ELEMENTS OF DEVELOPING STRATEGIES

Developing sound strategies generally involves the following:

Doing the right thing, not doing the wrong thing right When you don't make a proper analysis or set the right goals, you can wind up having the right strategies but for the wrong thing. That's why it is so important to go through the process carefully, diligently, thoroughly, honestly, and thoughtfully.

Determining the kind of organization you want to be What you do, which reflects your strategies, determines how your company will be seen by all the stakeholders. Strategies, therefore, can and do change perceptions.

Establishing the priorities and business mix The strategies you choose, the priorities you set for them, and your sustaining these priorities determine where you will put your resources, what your emphasis will be, and ultimately how your business mix will be dictated.

Deciding on the scope of operations Most people or enterprises want to become as big as they can. Seldom do they quantify what "big" is. Since every operation has physical limitations and finite resources, the strategies selected will, in fact, determine the scope. Consideration must be given to the effect your strategy will have on the desired scope of the operation.

Timing of major moves When you select certain strategies, set the timing of the moves you will make. It becomes very important to be aware of the effect that doing it now, or doing it at some other time, may have on your overall goals.

PLANNING AND STRATEGIZING NEVER END

Planning must be done, analyzed, re-planned, and done again. Most people plan on an annual basis, but there is nothing sacred about this period of time.

Review Your Plans Regularly It is a good idea to review your plans on some regular basis. When you re-plan, everything depends on what you are planning for and the environment within which you are operating.

Some things that trigger immediate review and possible re-planning are:

- An action by a competitor
- A major change in the marketplace
- A new threat from the economy
- New opportunities from the economy
- Financial problems
- Goals or strategies that don't seem to be working
- Changes by suppliers
- A change in your personal needs
- A major change in organizational direction

WHAT FIRST—STRATEGIZE OR ANALYZE?

Actually, you set your strategies from your goals, but you must also set strategies from assumptions made and from careful analysis.

Most people start by listing strategies for their goals, as I suggest, then, after the strategies are listed, review their strategies by checking the assumptions made. Most important: Do a SWOT analysis. SWOT is an acronym for Strengths, Weaknesses, Opportunities, and Threats. Lesson 10 tells you all about the SWOT analysis.

In this lesson you learned how to set strategies in order to achieve your goals, the characteristics of a strategic decision, the definition of circular planning, and why planning never ends. In the next lesson you learn how to analyze your situation, what SWOT is, and how to do a SWOT analysis.

LESSON 10

Analyzing Your Situation

In this lesson you learn how to analyze your situation, what SWOT is, and how to do a SWOT analysis.

SWOT Analysis—A Great Planning Tool

The SWOT analysis is the best tool for analyzing your internal and external environments within which you will be operating.

One of the major steps in planning is creating an analysis of *Strengths, Weaknesses, Opportunities,* and *Threats* (a *SWOT analysis*). Certo and Peter state in their book, *Strategic Management: A Focus On Process*, that "SWOT analysis is a useful tool for analyzing an organization's overall situation… This approach attempts to balance the internal strengths and weaknesses of an organization with opportunities and threats that the external environment presents."

In our consulting work we start every assignment that involves planning with an examination of the internal environment. We execute what we call an internal audit or analysis. This analysis provides an understanding of the organization's people and its financial, marketing, technological, production, administration, and other resources. This same internal environment analysis needs to be done by you.

Internal Environment All that involves what your organization is, what its resources are, how it operates, and anything else that is within the organization.

SWOT Analysis Criteria

Following is a checklist of some important internal environment factors. Exploring these topics is helpful in performing a SWOT analysis:

Financial Strengths and Weaknesses:

Do the financial goals and strategies tie in with the organization's vision and mission?

Cash flow

Break even needs

Profits

Best returns on investments

Borrowing power and payback ability

People Strengths and Weaknesses:

Do the people's goals and strategies tie in with the organization's vision and mission?

Specialized talents

Ability to lead and manage

Learning abilities

Relations with labor

Training

Pay scale and incentives

Absenteeism

Turnover rate

Production and Productivity:

Do the production and productivity goals and strategies tie in with the organization's vision and mission?

Efficiency

Controls

Layout of plant or system for providing services

Purchasing ability and power

Finding the right sources

Partnering

Marketing and Sales:

Do the marketing and sales goals and strategies tie in with the organization's vision and mission?

Distribution patterns

To whom you're selling what products

Pricing strategy

Advertising and promotional approaches

Which customers give you 80 percent of your business?

What niches are or are not being served?

I am sure you will think of other areas within your organization to appraise for strengths and weaknesses.

One Vision If you find that the people within your organization do not hold the same vision, mission, and goals, you're headed for big trouble.

DON'T JUMP HIGHER THAN YOUR HEAD

Too often an individual's or organization's aspirations are not realistic in light of the resources available. It is most important in the planning process to know this as soon as possible. A great deal of time and money can be spent pursuing unrealistic goals instead of those goals that would correct deficiencies so that your vision can be successfully pursued. The internal audit also gives you an understanding of who the key players are within the organization, and their perceptions of the organization and its activities. Through the audit you also gain a historical perspective that permits you to measure actual organizational activities against commonly accepted wisdom. You can then determine if the stated goals are shared and if they reflect a grasp of the organization's current situation.

To guide you in doing an internal analysis similar to what a consultant would do in using the SWOT technique, consider these broad-based questions:

- **What are your people's resources and capabilities?** What skills do they have? Do they match what is needed to achieve your goals?
- **What financial resources do you need to fuel the actions to achieve your goals?** Even if you have the resources, are they best invested in a particular goal or goals? What should be your financial priorities?
- **What are the organization's paradigms, and should they and can they be broken?** If you cannot change people's mental sets or the archetypes that govern the organization, change will not be possible.
- **Is there an atmosphere that encourages individual growth and change?** The organization's culture must be conducive to and encourage people to exhibit creativity and growth.
- **What are the resources and capabilities for various disciplines within the organization?** Can the people within the company objectively analyze resources and capabilities? If they can't, how will they measure their resources and capabilities in establishing benchmarks to reach and exceed?
- **Is there unanimous agreement regarding the company's strengths, weaknesses, opportunities, threats, prospects, goals, strategies, and direction?** Too often the decision-makers in companies, when individually asked to list company goals, will not list the same ones. Obviously a

company is in grave trouble when its people—and particularly its leaders—are not all pulling toward the same goals.

- **Are personal goals in synch with organizational goals?** If individual goals do not tie in with organizational goals, there is not likely to be shared vision or agendas.
- **Are new ideas encouraged?** What is done with them? How are the people who develop them treated? Are ideas in fact forthcoming? Is there direction toward the creative process? Are the new ideas tied to the goals?
- **What business are you in?** Do the people perceive you are in the business you think you are in? If you are not clear about the business you are in, you may well develop false goals.
- **What are the critical issues for the organization?** If you don't know your critical issues, how will you be able to marshal resources to deal with or support them?
- **What kind of management team do you have?** Do they have the skills and know-how to help you to achieve your vision, mission, and goals? Where do you have to cut back? Where must you add?
- **Is the organization meeting its financial objectives?** Quantifying and studying organizational statistics are important quantitative means of measuring the organization's progress.

Insiders Can Be Biased The internal SWOT, more than the external, can be readily prejudiced when done by people within the company. In order to develop as objective an analysis as possible, it is best to have the internal SWOT done by an outside source.

THE EXTERNAL ENVIRONMENT—THE BACK HALF OF SWOT

My own feeling is that you can apply the complete SWOT (strengths, weaknesses, opportunities, and threats) to both internal and external analysis. Most academicians, however, say that the strengths and weaknesses apply to the internal analysis and the opportunities and threats to the external analysis. Either way, the important thing is to do as complete an analysis as possible.

Internal Environment The circumstances, objectives, and conditions that surround you inside your company.

External Environment The circumstances, objectives, and conditions of the markets within which you will be competing.

The external environment is not something you can control. Knowing what you face, however, gives you the ability to adjust your organization to the changing external environment.

Following are some of the external environment's variables that you must examine and keep track of:

Competition

Customers and potential customers

Environmental factors

Government regulations on all levels

Political shifts

Social or cultural changes

Technological changes

The economy

Sleep with One Eye Open If you don't constantly monitor external factors, especially competition, you will be in for some big and unpleasant surprises.

You can hire consultants or research firms to provide primary research studies that give you information on any or all of the various external factors. This kind of information is useful but also expensive. Of course, not every external factor needs extensive research. You have to decide what factors will impact and affect your organization.

Many external factors can be researched by secondary research methods. It too can be done by a consultant or research firm, but it can also be done by you.

Primary Research Going to the source and directly generating the information you need, such as asking your customers what they think of a product or trend.

Secondary Research Obtaining the information from various sources who have already gathered the information you seek, such as a trade magazine that gives the size of a particular market.

Following is a list of some key secondary research sources:

10K reports on public corporations

Agencies at all levels of government

Business publications

Census Bureau

Customers

Customs Service

Department of Commerce

Newspapers

Published studies

Internet

Trade magazines

Trade organizations

Trade shows

Yearly financial statements of public corporations

Monitor External Forces Often External influences will constantly and heavily affect your organization and must be tracked on an ongoing basis.

Table 10.1 will help you in analyzing your strengths, weaknesses, opportunities, and threats, and it shows some examples of each.

TABLE 10.1 A SAMPLE SWOT WORKSHEET

STRENGTHS	WEAKNESSES
Mature management	Mature management
(This can be a weakness and a strength)	
Strong financial position	No line of credit
Good reputation	No new products
THREATS	**OPPORTUNITIES**
Technology is changing	Technology is changing
(This can be an opportunity and a threat)	
New environmental laws	Customers' growth
Buying power in hands of customers and they are dictating terms and price	Develop new products
Database direct marketing	

Brainstorm Before Research Before you do any research, write down all you can think of under each of the four SWOT categories. Have your key people do the same. Chart and compare the results. The lists give you a picture of how you and your people perceive your internal and external environments.

In this lesson you learned how to analyze your situation, what SWOT is, and how to do a SWOT analysis. In the next lesson you learn why the elements of a plan must come together, the functional areas of an organization, different management structures, and who the plan will impact.

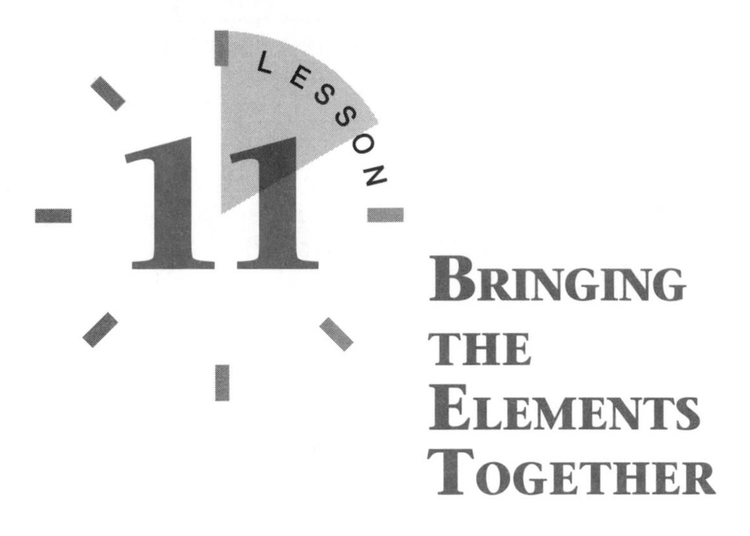

Bringing the Elements Together

In this lesson you learn why the elements of a plan must come together, the functional areas of an organization, different management structures, and who the plan will impact.

Five Fingers and a Fist

The various elements of a plan have to come together just as your five fingers do to make a fist. When they work together they can strike your objectives with impact. To achieve this you not only have to know what you're planning, but also who you're planning for. This kind of planning is called "Strategic Management," as it marshals your resources to accomplish your goals.

Strategic Management A process aimed at keeping an organization's resources matched to the internal and external environments in which it operates.

If you've followed the exercises in the previous lessons, all the elements will have to come together to form the written document—the plan. In previous lessons we spoke of developing your vision, mission, goals, and strategies. We also spoke of utilizing a SWOT analysis as an analytical tool in order to analyze both the internal environment of your organization and the external environment that you will be operating within. Future lessons address other elements such as the situation analysis, barriers, and core competencies. All these elements of the plan must come together to give rise to a cohesive whole.

Don't Write a Book Unfortunately too many plans wind up in someone's drawer and not actively used. Plans should be long enough to cover the subject but not so long that they won't get used.

In the early 1900s a Frenchman named Henri Fayol was a coal mine operator. He made his money by coordinating various functions, such as production and distribution, with sales into three markets—homes, factories, and steamships. He was one of the first to recognize the need to coordinate all the functions of his business. Before that the managers of each function followed their own goals. In developing your plan, whether you are a one-person operation, a small company, or a Fortune 500 company, your planning will be most effective if it takes into account all functions. You need to bring each function into the overall process and you need each functional area to plan on how to best support your organizational vision, mission, goals, and strategies.

Functions or **Functional Areas** Refers to the actions in a specialized area that contribute to the larger action of the organization. Major functional areas of an organization would be finance, marketing, production, and so on.

Each organization has functional areas that may be unique to it. It may combine those areas in different ways or single them out as full functions. The following is a list of general functional areas:

Production, manufacturing, or creating a service

Finance

Marketing

Customer service

Purchasing

New product development

Research and development

Technical services

Human resources

and others specific to your needs.

Segmented Plans Are Best Some people will only read the executive summary of your plan. Others will read the basic plan and still others will read the entire package. That is why it is a good idea to break the plan into segments, separating out all the supporting information into an appendix. More about it in Lesson 16.

Organizational Structures

As I have said, the various elements of the plan have to tie together within the structure that your organization uses. Based on the analysis of organizational structures described in Certo and Peter's book, *Strategic Management: A Focus On Process*, there are five major types of organizational structures. They are listed in the following sections.

The Simplest

You may use the simplest structure when you are the boss and you have an employee or employees working and reporting directly to you. With a simple structure you have the advantage of directly planning with the people who work with you. Decision-making is rapid and flexible.

Functional

The functional approach has each major functional area reporting to the Chief Executive Officer (CEO). It takes advantage of specialization and delegates the day-to-day activities. It tends to retain decision making under central control.

Divisional

The Divisional structure is usually used in larger organizations where it is necessary to break into groupings for better control. The division managers report to the CEO and all others within the division report to the division manager. This structure has the advantage of placing decision-making closer to where things happen, at the division level.

STRATEGIC BUSINESS UNIT

Some organizations grow to such a large degree that they break out their divisions under Strategic Business Units (SBUs). It is more like having businesses within the overall business. Here there is a vice president or president that leads each SBU. The division managers report to the head of the SBU. This structure facilitates the coordination of activities between divisions and tends to have in-depth planning within the SBU.

MATRIX

The most complex is a Matrix structure. The Matrix structure has a report area but also responsibility to other areas in the company. It permits cutting across lines and helps teams to work effectively.

An organization can use a variety of structures. It is within your chosen structure that your plan will be developed, applied, and implemented. Just as all functions need to be considered and involved when planning, so too must the type of management structure be considered.

Goods and Services The major difference between marketing a product and marketing a service is that the service is created at the same time it is consumed. There is no taking back the service as there is in a product when the user is dissatisfied or it doesn't work.

WHO WILL BE IMPACTED BY THE PLAN?

Who will use your plan? This depends on people's involvement in its development and the practical application it has for them in terms of their responsibilities and function.

Naturally, everyone who is in your organization and deals with it will be impacted. But a great deal of how you structure your plan depends on who will be using the plan and what it will be used for. After all, a plan is nothing more than a document representing well thought-out objectives and critical views of your organization's overall direction. It is obviously something you'll want to communicate to others. It also has other uses which we cover in the next lesson.

The Elements Change, but the Process Remains In each plan you may utilize a different group of planning elements. The basic planning process, however, is the same.

Within the overall business plan are many sub-plans. There are also plans for various functions within the organization and for use outside of the organization.

There are plans for the following facets of your organization:

- Your overall organization—the "Grand Plan"
- The strategic direction of your organization—which can be part of or in place of the "Grand Plan"

- Various functions within the organization, such as management, marketing, finance, production, customer service, and so on
- Obtaining money from outside sources
- Managing your money
- Managing your people
- Operations of a department
- An event such as attending a trade show
- Establishing the operation of a factory
- Laying out your customer service operation
- Selling your products and/or services
- Determining if a business or new product is worth going into

And much more that you will think of as you read on.

In this lesson we learned about the elements of a plan and how they must come together, the functional areas of an organization, different management structures, and who the plan will impact. In the next lesson you learn about additional tools you will need to develop your plan, what business you are in, and targeting customers.

LESSON 12

Analytical Tools for Developing Your Plan

In this lesson you learn about tools you need to develop your plan, knowing what business you are in, and targeting customers.

Tools for Developing the Plan

The organization's written plan incorporates vision, mission, goals, and strategies. You used a SWOT Analysis, described in Lesson 10, as an analytical tool. In addition, you should use other tools in developing your plan. Basically these tools are questions that need to be answered in order to complete your analysis and lay down your plan. They are:

- What business are you in?
- Who are your target customers?
- What markets will you operate within?
- Who is your competition?
- What are the financial and people resources you will need?

- What are the products and/or services you will offer?
- What are your core competencies?
- Have you done a situational analysis?
- What are the barriers you need to overcome?

Don't Move Too Soon Don't move ahead with a plan unless you have a clear picture or understanding of what should be done and why you should do it. Gathering the information that answers the questions just listed should give you the answers.

WHAT BUSINESS ARE YOU IN?

A probing question that you need to ask is, "What business are we in?" It should be asked in relation to your organization's overall activities as well as for your strategic business unit, division, department, group, team, or whatever area you are working in. An organization or functional group that knows the business they are in can better plan their action. It helps in establishing missions, goals, strategies, objectives, tactics, criteria, and the arenas in which you will do business.

Don't Be Afraid to Ask As an individual you should be asking yourself the question, "What business am I in?" If you, as an individual, know the business you're in you can more readily plan your career and know what it is that your organization expects of you. You might ask, "What business am I in, in delivering what the boss wants?"

A client of ours, Hercules Chemical Company, Inc., represents a good example of how asking, "What business are you in?" can lead to growth and to achieving organizational goals.

A major goal Hercules had was to obtain specific dollar growth through new product development, acquisition, and market development.

Since they were selling some products into the janitorial supply, automotive chemical, and hardware industries, they explored ways to expand into these areas.

In order to focus their resources and efforts, we asked the question, "What business are you in?" Each executive had a different answer and named a different business they thought Hercules was in. Businesses named were plumbing, manufacturing, chemicals, and distribution. They each had good reasons to select the business they did.

If, however, we could define and agree upon the business Hercules is or should be in, they would know where to focus their efforts and resources.

We started to analyze the situation. 95 percent of their business came from selling chemicals to the plumbing industry. The company sales people and independent sales reps called on the plumbing trade. Their many warehouses around the country stocked products for only that trade and for all the products they manufactured, and, with a few exceptions, were primarily for that trade.

In order to obtain a clearer understanding of the company's strengths and weaknesses as well as the market opportunities and threats, we did a SWOT analysis. We also looked at Hercules' history and culture. These helped us answer the following questions:

- Who are our customers and target customers?
- What equipment do we have and what can it produce?
- What are the strengths of our distribution network?
- What markets would be most profitable?
- What are our core competencies?
- How effective is our competition?
- What resources do we have available to invest in growth?

This in-depth analysis was then put together into a written *situational analysis.*

Situational Analysis An analysis of how the organization is placed in relation to its surroundings.

Our conclusion was that Hercules' greatest strengths, the company culture, core competencies, opportunity for profits, and so on clearly placed them in the *plumbing chemical business*.

Knowing that Hercules was in the plumbing chemical business gave them the direction they needed for new product development, the type of acquisition to target, and markets in which to concentrate their distribution. It has led to a clear and successful direction for growth.

Don't Get Lost in Details In planning you can get lost in what seems like an awful lot of detail. Don't let it overwhelm you. You need only take from the planning process what applies to your situation.

Who Are Your Target Customers?

You want to be able to target in on the customers and potential customers who can produce the most profitable revenue for the organization. If you are a not-for-profit organization you will be targeting the customers who can provide the most resources (donations) as well as the customer who will derive the most benefit from your organization's activities.

Internal Customers

If you are working within an organization you have internal customers to serve. For example, if you are a researcher, your internal customer might be the marketing managers, pricing people, sales organization, or some other group. By satisfying these internal customers you help them provide the product or services that the paying customers will buy.

Paying Customers

The most important thing is to clearly identify and target the paying customers. If you don't know who you want to sell to, then you won't know the following important strategies and characteristics:

- How to marshal your resources
- What products to develop
- The services to offer
- How best to reach your customers
- Who your customers are

- Prospective targets
- How many targets there are
- The buying patterns of your paying customers

You also must have a clear understanding of your customer's needs in order to satisfy what your customer wants.

Needs and **Wants** Needs are what the product or service functionally satisfies for the customer. Wants are the emotional desire for something. For example, I *want* a hole in a piece of steel but, I *need* a certain kind of drill that can go through steel and make a certain size hole.

KNOW YOUR CUSTOMER BASE

You should know what your customer base is and what you want it to be.

In dealing in the consumer goods area, you need to know the customers that you want to reach. What do you know about your customers in the following areas?

Age	Education
Income	Where they live
Gender	Size of family
Occupation	And so on

These and other similar characteristics are called *demographics*. You also need to know the customers' *psychographics*, that is, their lifestyle.

For example, do they like:

Camping	Music
Sports	Home activities
Theater	Eating out
Books	Technology

And so on.

Demographics and **Psychographics** The statistics profile and the lifestyle of your customers and potential customers.

In dealing with industrial, commercial, or other business-to-business situations, you must also know the profile of your customers and their distribution patterns. The questions at the end of this lesson will help you to draw up a profile for each customer and for your customer base in general.

How Will You Reach Your Customers?

You must know a good deal about your customers and potential customers in order to figure out how best to reach them.

You might sell:

- Directly to the consumer or end user
- To a retailer
- To a distributor who in turn sells to a retailer who then sells to the consumer or end user

See the Basic Distribution Chart in Figure 12.1 for a graphic illustration.

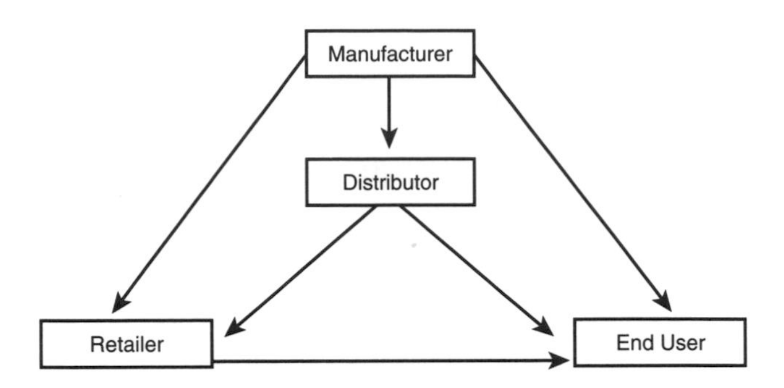

Figure 12.1 The Basic Distribution Chart.

All of those in the chain of distribution are your customers, directly or indirectly. You need to profile them and understand the markets they make up. We discuss more about this in the next lesson.

Know Your Customers The more you know about your customers the better you can satisfy their needs.

To help get a clear understanding of who your customers are, ask yourself the following:

- Who are my customers?
- Who are my potential customers?
- What do they buy from me?
- What would I like them to buy from me?
- Where are they located?
- What are their wants and needs?
- Who makes the buying decision?

- When do they do the buying and in what cycle?
- How do they buy?
- Where do they buy?

In this lesson you learned about the tools you need to develop your plan, knowing what business you are in, and targeting customers. In the next lesson you learn about markets, competition, resources, products and services, situation analysis, core competencies, and overcoming barriers.

LESSON 13

More Analytical Tools

In this lesson you learn about markets, competition, resources, products and services, situation analysis, core competencies, and overcoming barriers.

What Markets Will You Operate Within?

Just as in the Hercules example in Lesson 12, in which the company executives had to decide what business they were in, you must also decide on what markets you want to focus.

Market is the location of a demand or a potential demand for particular products and services. The markets are an assembly of potential customers.

To help you decide which markets should get your attention, consider the following questions:

- Who are the 20 percent of the customers that give you 80 percent of your business?
- What do your key customers buy and what do they want to buy?
- How can you clearly segment your markets in the following categories?

Geography	Trade	Size	Growth
Product	Volume	Profitability	

- What are your marketing and sales costs for each market you sell to?
- What products or services are giving you 80 percent of your business?
- Who is the competition?
- What distribution structures are available?
- What is the size of the market by dollars, product, units, or other measures?
- If consumer-oriented, what arc the demographics and psychographics?
- If business-to-business, what are the buying customs and practices?

The 80/20 Rule The old 80/20 rule works in almost every situation. It suggests that 20 percent of your customers are responsible for 80 percent of your business and profits. You should focus on that group of customers.

WHO IS YOUR COMPETITION?

Competition is anyone who offers products or services that are the same or similar to what you offer. They pursue the same customers and probably the same markets as you. You, therefore, should have a continuous method for monitoring what these people are doing.

Everyone in your organization must be sensitive to what the competition is doing. They should be alert not only to competitive activity, but have a means of reporting what they hear and see to a central keeper of competitive information. The central keeper should gather the following information from each competitor:

Catalogs	Advertising
Price sheets	Trade show handouts
Rumors	Community activities
Financial information	Want ads

and anything else that gives you a full picture of each of your competitors.

Competition Has Many Faces Your competition comes from people and organizations who make products or services that directly compete with you and also from anything that takes money away from what would otherwise have gone to you.

Your external environmental analysis should have produced your initial information on your competition. You will, however, want to keep the information as up-to-date as possible.

To help you do that, here are some of the best sources for competitive information:

Customers	Trade journals
Your sales people	Trade associations
Suppliers	Trade shows

Public companies' annual reports and 10K reports

What Are the Financial and People Resources You Will Need?

Too often organizations develop grand plans, but they neglect to tie them to the reality of the resources they have available.

The dollars you can afford to risk, as well as the talent of the people available, should be a major factor in your planning.

People have often come to us with a very good product or service they invested their last risk dollars to develop. They are desperate to get their creation sold. But with no more dollars left, they cannot market the product themselves and often have to sell, license, or find someone else to market it for them. They have put themselves in the position of building a great car, so to speak, but with no money for gas to drive it. If, on top of the lack of dollar resources, they don' t have someone with the skill to drive or maintain the car, then they also lack people resources.

Try Teamwork When you do not have the resources, you can sometimes partner with another organization to achieve your objectives.

When you do not have the people resources your plan calls for, you can reach out to many organizations or people who are in the specialized businesses of providing certain resources.

Following is a list of some skills and services you can obtain from outside of your organization:

Bookkeeping	Phone answering	Accounting
Secretarial	Legal	Consulting in almost any area
Data processing	Payroll processing	Independent sales Reps
Office space	Marketing	Design

The list could go on for pages.

In order to evaluate your resources ask yourself these questions:

- What skills do we need?
- What skills do our people have?
- Where can I obtain the skills that we don't have?
- What would it cost to develop the skills we need?
- Realistically now, what are the dollars we need?
- Are the dollars needed on a cyclical or steady basis?
- What is the least likely, most likely, and best possible return of money that I can expect?

What Are the Products and/or Services You Will Offer?

If you know your customer and your own ability to produce products or services for them, you will know the areas for which you should be developing products and services. Don't just think, however, in terms of your machinery or what you can produce. Think also in terms of your customers' needs. Even if you can't produce for particular needs, you may be able to offer the product or service by partnering with another organization. Today such partnering is very prevalent.

Differential Advantage The advantage you can gain by having something that is different from the competition and adds value to your product or service in the customers' eyes.

Here are some questions you should ask yourself about your product or services when doing your planning:

- What is the differential advantage that my product or service has over everyone else?
- What are the features and benefits of each of my offerings?
- What is the competition offering?
- What does a comparative analysis of competitors' offerings and ours show?

- What are the wants and needs of the consumer or end user?
- How much of it can we sell?
- What will our profits be?
- How long will it take to obtain a return from our investment in a particular product or service?
- What is our return on investment (ROI)?

WHAT ARE YOUR CORE COMPETENCIES?

Core competencies are probably the factors least examined or recognized by management. Even worse, core competencies needed to move into new areas of opportunity are rarely analyzed. World-class companies have a thorough understanding of their core competencies and have aligned them with their strategies in order to leverage these competencies. In order to understand the required core competencies, you need to know the market arenas in which you intend to compete. Ultimately, the core competencies have to exist on multidisciplinary levels. You must possess the competency, the customer must perceive that you have the competency, and you must be better at it than your competition.

Core Competencies What the organization is best at doing. The integral capabilities, skills, and knowledge that drive the company.

HAVE YOU DONE A SITUATION ANALYSIS?

As we said in the last lesson, a situational analysis is an analysis of how the organization is placed in relation to its surroundings. In order to arrive at such an analysis, you must look at your internal and external situation at the time you are doing the planning. You should have done your SWOT analysis and asked many of the questions posed in this and the last lesson. Now is the time to put together the information learned into a broad overview or picture—the situation analysis. You do this so that anyone who reads your plan will understand the reasons behind your recommendations—in other words, where you are coming from, what the situation is, and why it calls for the actions and schedules that you have set forth.

Conduct a Situational Analysis The situational analysis examines where you stand in relation to your industry, as well as in relation to world-class performance, regardless of industry.

WHAT ARE THE BARRIERS YOU NEED TO OVERCOME?

The most obvious barriers that prevent your organization from achieving your goals may be recognized but more subtle ones may not. Direct competition may be the first barrier pointed out. In fact, a more important barrier might be the lack of an effective distribution network. The important thing, as you work on your plan, is to recognize what the barriers may be so that you can best plan how to overcome them.

Barriers Impediments that stand in the way of your accomplishing what you want to achieve.

If you look to all the weaknesses that you developed in doing your SWOT analysis, you will unearth many of the barriers you have to face.

Some common barriers that most organizations face are:

- Lack of resources, both financial and people
- Overburdened staff
- Competition
- Lack of the right distribution system
- No strategic direction established by upper management
- A lack of understanding of customer needs
- Resistance from the corporate culture
- Lack of infrastructure to support the plan

In this lesson you learned about markets, competition, resources, products and services, situation analysis, core competencies, and overcoming barriers. In the next lesson you learn how to think strategically.

Strategic Thinking and Leadership

In this lesson you learn what strategic thinking is, the four keys to strategic thinking, how to act strategically, why it's important to lead, characteristics of leadership, and some good books on leadership.

What Is Strategic Thinking?

Strategic thinking not only helps you to develop a focused plan that takes into account your internal and external situations, but it also enables you to act strategically when you implement your plan.

Strategic Thinking Knowing where you want to aim, the resources you need to strike the target, the conditions that surround the target, and how you will hit it.

Some people are born strategic thinkers. Others have to develop a faculty for thinking in strategic terms. If you feel that you do not think strategically, here are four keys that you must make part of your mental set. If you are a strategic thinker, the four keys are for your review.

HAVE A VISION

A strategic thinker has a vision or a dream to lead people toward. It does not matter if you are developing a plan for your own life, or for an organization, division, department, section, group, or whatever. Without being able to clearly envision the purpose of your plan, you will not be able to lead others in its implementation. They too, must understand and share the vision of what the plan represents. The fortunate person has a vision—a dream.

KNOW YOUR RESOURCES

It is one thing to have a vision; it is quite another to realistically know if you have the wherewithall, the resources, to achieve it. Sometimes when you analyze your resources you may find they are not sufficient to achieve your vision. It doesn't mean, necessarily, that you have to give up your vision. Rather, it means you will have to use whatever resources you now have to take steps toward the vision while you build or acquire additional resources. The wise person knows her strengths and weaknesses.

UNDERSTAND THE PLAYING FIELD

Always think in terms of the external environment, or "playing field," within which the plan will be implemented. A good player knows the "playing field" and knows the opportunities and threats it presents.

Playing Field The arena or external environment within which you operate. It is where competition resides and where economic, social, government, and all other factors out there impact on what you do.

To help you analyze the arena or "playing field," you should ask yourself the following questions:

- What will motivate those on the playing field to perform the action I want?
- Why should those on the playing field react to my plan?
- When will the things happen that I want to happen?
- How will they react to my plan?
- Where do I have to place my resources?
- Who are all the players that can affect me?

Rudyard Kipling's Six Questions

As you saw under the previous key, I have applied six questions to understanding the "playing field." These questions should be applied to analyze any and all situations. The strategic thinker examines everything under the light of: what, why, when, how, where, and who.

Inquisition (the Good Kind) "I keep six honest serving-men (They taught me all I knew); Their names are What and Why and When and How and Where and Who." From *The Elephant's Child,* Stanza I by Rudyard Kipling.

LEADERSHIP AND STRATEGIC THINKING

Most leaders are strategic thinkers. They have a vision of what they want to do, know what they have to work with, and know how they want it done. They are able to analyze situations and evoke confidence, trust, and respect. It is the leader who gets things done.

It is very difficult to obtain backing for your plans or to implement them unless you can exercise leadership. Leaders are almost always strategic thinkers. In today's organizational environment it is more and more often assumed that each individual will be a strategic planner and a leader. Central strategic planning departments are going from doing all the planning to being the coordinators, orchestrators, and resources suppliers, so that everyone, at every level, can do his own strategic planning for his activities.

Try To Do Both For you to plan and have someone else do the implementing is never as effective as having *those that plan implement, and those that implement plan.*

WHAT IS LEADERSHIP?

I did a small study of leadership for New York University's Business Leadership Committee, of which I am member. The survey involved thirty people in five countries. Here are the consolidated responses to the five questions we asked.

Leadership The ability to get people to follow someone toward a specific goal.

THE DEFINING QUALITIES OF LEADERSHIP

The ability to get people to follow one toward a specific goal is seen as a defining quality of a leader. Just as important, though, is a sense of vision—the ability to see the big picture—and perhaps the ability to anticipate the picture before it becomes visible to the average eye. Another frequently mentioned defining quality is respect—more specifically, the ability to command respect from those whom one is leading. Honesty, an air of confidence, character, and integrity were also mentioned.

CHARACTERISTICS INHERENT TO A LEADER

The most frequently mentioned characteristics were vision, charisma, fairness, ethical and moral strength, and intelligence. Also mentioned were the ability to communicate, honesty, energy, empathy, confidence, and the courage to stand up for one's beliefs.

THE BEST LEADERSHIP BOOK YOU CAN RECOMMEND

The responses ranged from Tom Peters' and Robert H. Waterman, Jr.'s *In Search of Excellence* to the Bandler and Grinder series on neurolinguistic programming, and from

The Man Who Changed The World (Gail Sheehy's book on Gorbachev) to *How To Win Friends and Influence People* by Dale Carnegie. Others included *The Whole Manager* (Dennis P. Slavin, Ph.D.) and *Leadership and the One-Minute Manager* (Blanchard).

Mark Bobrow, compiler of this study, added the following observations: "If I may add a cultural pragmatist's view: The first one a leader must lead, of course, is himself/herself. That is, leadership comes first from within. At the same time, though, leadership is a socio-cultural construct. It is the convergence of individual vision—influenced, to be sure, by social and cultural contexts—and the historical/cultural moment that, for better or worse, produces effective leaders. I can think of no better articulation of the qualities, habits of mind, vision, and potential dangers (both individual and societal) of what is here being called leadership than the essays of Ralph Waldo Emerson (particularly *Self-Reliance, Circles,* and *The American Scholar),* the journals of Henry David Thoreau (including *Walden*), and the work of William James (especially *Pragmatism* and *The Varieties of Religious Experience.*)"

CAN LEADERSHIP BE TAUGHT?

Most survey participants felt that leadership skills (such as openness, honesty, and communication) can be taught, refined, or enhanced, but that there are certain qualities inherent in a leader, such as vision and charisma, that cannot be taught. One response suggested that while it may be possible to bring out dormant leadership characteristics, it is not possible to create those characteristics in an individual. Nor, it should be added, does it seem possible to teach someone to have the will to lead.

IS LEADERSHIP REPLACING MANAGEMENT OR AUGMENTING IT?

Responses to this question were fairly divided. Some felt that leadership is replacing management, others felt it is enhancing management, and still others felt that leadership neither replaces nor augments management, but rather complements it. One respondent said that the two are different sides of the same coin, that one must "recognize [those] situations that call for management and those that call for leadership and be able to move comfortably between the two." Another suggested that management is being "gutted" from organizations, and that what often passes for leadership is nothing more than "plain, old-fashioned, unadulterated greed."

My own feeling is that leadership and management are blending. There is a great need for managers who are leaders, and that is what corporate America is looking for.

In this lesson you learned what strategic thinking is, the four keys to strategic thinking, how to act strategically, why it's important to lead, characteristics of leadership, and some good books on leadership. In the next lesson you learn why you need contingency planning, contingencies for high priority areas, contingency planning for scheduling, five benefits of contingency planning, and seven steps to contingency planning.

LESSON 15

Contingency Planning

In this lesson you learn why you need contingency planning, contingencies for high priority areas, contingency planning for scheduling, five benefits of contingency planning, and the seven steps to contingency planning.

Why You Need Contingency Planning

Plans deal with what you expect to happen. But no matter how well you plan, the unexpected can and often does take place. Sometimes the unexpected is a favorable event and other times it may be unfavorable.

During the Christmas 1996 buying season, demand for the Tickle Me Elmo doll completely eclipsed the manufacturer's expectations. It was certainly a favorable reaction to a new product. Nevertheless, the planned production was far below the demand and so the product was in short supply. If, on the other hand, consumers had rejected Elmo, that unfavorable response would probably have left the manufacturer with huge overruns. In either case, the company would have had to put contingency plans into effect.

Contingency Something that is likely but not certain to happen.

YOU CAN'T PLAN FOR EVERY CONTINGENCY

There is no way you can plan for every contingency but you certainly can plan for most likely ones. In critical areas it is a good idea to build into your plans three levels of projections for key events and have contingencies worked out if the "most likely" scenario does not work out.

The three projections you should make in critical areas are:

- **The most likely**—What you think will actually happen.
- **The least likely**—The worse case you can imagine for what you are projecting.
- **The most optimistic**—The best possible scenario you can imagine if everything goes beyond your expectations.

Expect the Unexpected Even building in the three levels of possible projections does not always reflect reality. No matter how well you do your research, how thorough your SWOT and other analyses are, or how well thought out your assumptions, unexpected things will happen.

CONTINGENCIES FOR HIGH PRIORITY AREAS

Since it is impractical, if not impossible, to build contingencies into every area of your plan, you should concentrate only in the areas that are of high priority or are highly sensitive to change.

Some of the areas that might apply to your situation include the following:

- New competition entering or withdrawing from the market.
- Your projected sales volume is greatly under or over projection.
- Profits are off target.
- New technology appears.
- Disasters such as floods, earthquakes, tornadoes, hurricanes, and other acts of nature.
- Other disasters such as computer breakdowns, strikes, hostile take-over, and so on.
- Changing government regulations.

An Ounce of Prevention Milton (Mickey) Rosenau, Jr., in his book *Successful Project Management,* said, "Contingency can be thought of as the antidote of risk."

CONTINGENCIES FOR SCHEDULING

Scheduling is a major area where contingency planning must be used. What happens if a supplier does not deliver a key part on time or an approval needed from another functional area within your organization is not given as promised? What will you do? Think it out beforehand and have alternative plans available to put into action.

While writing this lesson I heard and read about America Online's problems in meeting huge demands by subscribers after the company offered a flat monthly fee with no time restrictions. Would this problem have been so severe if AOL had thought out the scheduling for integrating new customers into the system? I think not. They might have saved a major problem from developing if they had scheduled the phase-in of anticipated new customers and had contingencies for the best possible results to their new pricing strategy. Now they have to play catch-up.

Two Heads Are Better Than One Because you have to rely on others outside and within your organization, it is wise to insist that those you interact with develop contingencies, too.

Here are just a few scheduling scenarios that should have built-in contingencies. It is based on Roseanu's scheduling and cost contingency list.

- Your computer system goes down at a critical time or in the middle of a major project.
- Your supplier can't deliver on time.

- You can't deliver on time.
- The powers-that-be shift to a higher priority.
- The government issues new regulations.
- You are faced with a strike.
- An act of nature closes you down.
- A major fault shows up in one of your products or services.
- Vacations or illnesses affect scheduling.
- There is poor communication.
- There is a lack of approvals from various functional areas within the organization on time.

FIVE BENEFITS OF CONTINGENCY PLANNING

In case it's not yet obvious why you should do contingency planning, here are five benefits the process ensures:

- It makes everyone in your organization aware of how unpredictable the future can be.
- It helps train associates not to think in absolutes.
- If you expect the unexpected, you are less likely to panic and are more likely to react strategically.
- It puts you in a position to take advantage of unexpected opportunities.
- It prepares you to react to potential threats that become reality.

SEVEN STEPS TO CONTINGENCY PLANNING

As I said before, you can't have contingency plans for everything. However, you need to build into your plans contingencies for major areas. Here are seven steps that will help you.

1. Look over your opportunities and threats from your SWOT analysis and determine which will have major impact if they were to happen.
2. Use the opportunities and threats to indicate where you need contingency planning.
3. Establish a set of signs to watch for and to trigger planned reactions.
4. Estimate the benefit or harm that can happen should certain events take place. This helps you determine the major areas in which to establish contingency plans.
5. Be sure that whatever contingency plans you develop are true to your vision and mission.
6. Set up ways of monitoring for the unexpected.
7. Develop action plans for key events that may occur.

Don't Delay You had better start worrying—and then start planning—if you don't know what you would do if something bad happened. It means you have not done any thinking about contingency events.

In this lesson you learned why you need contingency planning, contingencies for high priority areas, contingency planning for scheduling, five benefits of contingency planning, and the seven steps to contingency planning. In the next lesson you learn how scheduling helps make things happen, why milestones are essential, and about scheduling devices, task schedules, software programs, and the war room.

LESSON 16

Scheduling—Where the Tire Hits the Road

In this lesson you will learn how scheduling helps make things happen, why milestones are essential, about scheduling devices, task schedules, software programs, and the war room.

Scheduling Is the "When" and "Who" of Making It Happen

It is all well and good to have plans, but someone has to turn the plans into action. By assigning individual responsibilities and specific times when certain things are to happen, a plan is moved from paper to reality. Scheduling completion dates sets the stage for when various actions have to take place and who will be responsible for making these actions happen.

Scheduling Establishing when you want things to happen and who will make them happen.

Scheduling can be as simple as putting dates in your calendar or as complex as formulating diagrams, charts, and tracking

THE TASK LIST IS IMPORTANT

It is a good idea to develop a detailed task list that supports the milestones. As they say, "the devil is in the details," and without detailing who will do what and when, your plan may not be successfully implemented. After all, it is the task list that supports the milestones.

Your task list should serve the following functions:

- List each and every task
- Indicate who will perform the task
- List a target date for completion

What Must Happen? In order to set forth the tasks needed to implement your plan, ask yourself what are the things you must do to make this plan work?

TYPES OF SCHEDULING DEVICES

There are many scheduling devices. Some are better for one area of planning and some for another. You will have to decide which is best for you.

TIME AND ACTIVITY CHART

Next to just putting dates in your calendar, a time and activity chart is the simplest device for scheduling. You break each objective or goal into tasks and assign a time when it is to be completed, a mini-milestone—if you will. Table 16.1 shows a Time and Activity chart for doing a Business Plan.

Your Results May Vary This Business Plan Time and Activity Chart will vary depending upon the complexity of your plan and its purpose. The example in Table 16.1 is a simple version.

TABLE 16.1 A BUSINESS PLAN TIME AND ACTIVITY CHART

TASKS AND MILESTONES	MONTHS											
DEVELOP YOUR BUSINESS PLAN	*1*	*2*	*3*	*4*	*5*	*6*	*7*	*8*	*9*	*10*	*11*	*12*
Develop your vision	X											
Draw up the mission		X										
Establish goals				X								
Set strategies				X								
Do SWOT analysis					X							
Review goals and strategies in light of SWOT							X					
Complete written plan				X								

Bar Chart

A bar chart, as shown in Figure 16.1, gives a graphic picture of how you are progressing by task, each task in relation to one another.

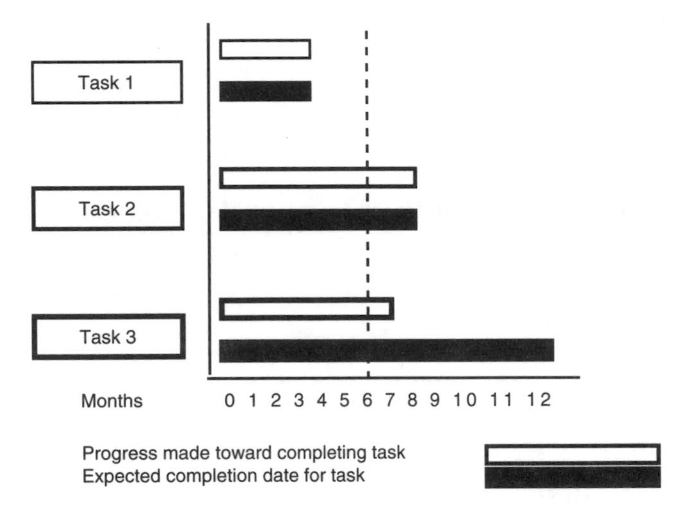

Figure 16.1 This bar chart compares actual progress against expected dates of completion.

The clear horizontal bar in Figure 16.1 represents the progress made for that activity and the black filled in bar indicates the target completion month. At a six-month review, indicated by the dotted vertical line, we can see the progress made for each activity based upon a twelve month time cycle. It shows that activity 1 is completed, on time. Activity 2 is completed ahead of time and activity 3 has five months until it must be completed.

Bar charts Often called Gantt charts.

Network Diagrams

Network diagrams are a more complex way of linking various tasks together to show their interdependence. They also give more information. Although they are more complex, they are an excellent way of seeing more complicated projects and interrelated tasks.

Three Varieties of Network Diagrams The three basic network diagrams are Program Evaluation and Review Technique (PERT), Precedence Diagramming Method (PDM), and Arrow Diagramming Method (ADM).

Different ways they may appear are shown in Figure 16.2:

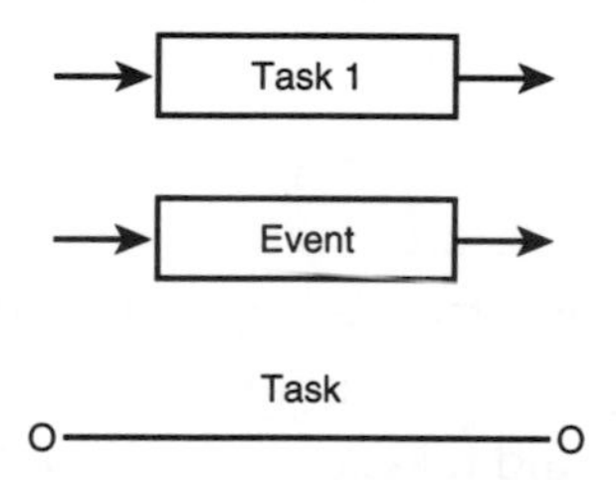

Figure 16.2 How network diagrams might appear.

The use of these various nodes and lines to indicate the task or event are put together in different ways depending on what is being planned. It is beyond the scope this book to go into details on this more complex but often used method of scheduling. Most books devoted to project management give a detailed description of the use of these charts.

For More Information An excellent detailed chapter on Network Diagrams is in Milton D. Rosenau, Jr.'s book, *Successful Project Management.*

THE WAR ROOM

Very often I suggest that clients set up a "War Room" in which a large chart is placed on the wall with a complete schedule of the project, tasks, milestones, completion dates, and so on. In that way, the project can be tracked and everyone can see the progress being made. The names of the individuals that are responsible for leading the task or activity to completion are also indicated on the wall chart. Use of such a chart has proven to be an excellent motivator that helps meet the deadline dates.

In this lesson you learned how scheduling helps make things happen, why milestones are essential, about scheduling devices, task-scheduling software programs, and the war room. In the next lesson you learn about the content of the written plan, the form it should take, questions to determine the form, how the plan comes together, and writing the plan.

LESSON 17

The Written Plan—Should Form Follow Function?

In this lesson you learn about the content of the written plan, the form it should take, questions to determine the form, how the plan comes together, and writing the plan.

What Form Produces the Best Results?

No one can tell you what form to use for your written plan in order to get the best results. It depends on who you will be presenting the plan to, who will be using it, and what you want the plan to accomplish.

If the plan is for a small working group, you might take a simple, straightforward approach. On the other hand, if the plan is for approval of the top executive committee of your organization, you will need to have a very complete and well thought-out written document. You also need a visual presentation (slide show) to present to the various groups that your plan will impact, along with detailed backup material to support your plan's presentations.

Form The shape or structure the plan takes.

DETERMINING FORM

Asking yourself or your team the following questions will help you to determine form:

Who is the plan for?

Is the plan for obtaining approval, for implementation, or both?

Is it to raise money?

Do you want to obtain buy-in from a particular group of people?

Will you be presenting the plan to groups?

Is visual impact important?

Will those who receive the plan only read the executive summary, read it in-depth, skim through it, or want all substantiating documentation?

The executive summary, mentioned in the last question, is discussed later in the lesson.

First Things First An old adage says that form should follow function. In other words, once you know what you want your plan to achieve, you can choose the best form to accomplish it.

THE MANY FACES OF FORM

The plan can take many different forms:

- A book form with all collateral material.
- A three-ring binder with clearly delineated sections.
- An unbound short report.
- Each section bound separately in modules so that the modules can be included or excluded, depending on who is viewing the presentation.
- A briefcase with the bound plan and the support material.

HOW THE PLAN COMES TOGETHER

In order to bring the plan together as a unified whole the content of the written plan should state the following things clearly:

- History and background—enough information that someone not familiar with your subject will understand where you are coming from.
- Your vision—what you envision your plan will ultimately achieve or support.
- Your mission—what you are asking people to set forth and do.
- Clear goals—what you want them to achieve.
- Your strategies—how you want them to achieve it.
- An explanation of your reasoning—why you want it done.
- Who will do it—assignments of responsibilities.

- When will it be done—schedule with milestones.
- What will it cost—budgets.
- Your expected results—what you will get for your investment of time and money.
- The method for monitoring and measuring results.

Know How to Define Success What will success be? If you don't all agree in advance what success will be, you will not know what to measure and monitor.

TYPICAL TOPICS OR SECTIONS TO INCLUDE IN YOUR PLAN

Here are examples of major sections that a written plan could contain. Not all plans will have every section nor does the list of possible sections represent every possibility. It is intended only to explain the major sections and reference possibilities that might trigger ideas of what to include in your plan.

Each Plan Is Different It is not likely that your plan will need all the topics or sections I have listed. Each plan will dictate different needs and therefore different contents.

COVER PAGE

Every plan should have a Cover Page and/or a Title Page. The cover page can be decorative with graphics that support the thrust or theme of the report, as shown in Figure 17.1.

Figure 17.1 An example of a corporate cover page.

Title Page

The Title Page contains all the pertinent detail that describes what the report is about. See Figure 17.2 for an example. The Title Page should, however, have certain basic information such as:

- The title of the report that describes what it covers
- The time period the plan covers
- The date of issue
- The writer(s)
- Contact information such as address, phone, fax, and e-mail
- The name of the organization
- A statement of confidentiality

Table of Contents

The Table of Contents is another must for every report. Positioned after the title page, it should provide easy reference to important topics. Often the table of contents' major topics are tabbed throughout the report making them easy to find.

You might list only major headings or sections in your table of contents, as in Figure 17.3, or you could list subheadings under each major category, as in Figure 17.4. The choice depends on the complexity of your plan. Obviously, the simple plan needs only major category lists, while the more complex one needs more detail in order to help the reader more easily find information.

The numbering of the pages can be sequential throughout the plan or each section of the plan can have its own numbers.

BOBROW CONSULTING GROUP, INC.

BUILDING FOR THE TWENTY-FIRST CENTURY

ANNUAL STRATEGIC PLAN

SEPTEMBER 1997
BORROW CONSULTING GROUP, INC.
CONFIDENTIAL DOCUMENT

Prepared by

Edwin E. Bobrow, CMC

BOBROW CONSULTING GROUP
10 MAIN STREET
ANYTOWN, STATE 54321
PHONE: 800-555-1234
FAX: 800-555-2345

Copyright 1998
All rights reserved.
The information contained in this document is confidential and proprietary. Any unauthorized use or distributionis strictly prohibited.

Figure 17.2 A sample title page.

Sample Tables of Contents Two examples of a possible Table of Contents will give you some idea of the forms it can take. You should do the Table of Contents after you have completed the report so that it reflects the headings and sections you have established in the final report.

A simple Table of Contents might be like that shown in Figure 17.3.

	Page
Preface	1
Executive Summary	3
Situational Analysis	6
Key Findings and Conclusions	8
Recommendations	11
References	15
Glossary	20
Appendices	25

Figure 17.3 A simple table of contents.

A more complex Table of Contents might resemble Figure 17.4.

Figure 17.4 A more complex table of contents.

EXECUTIVE SUMMARY

Just as the table of contents is done after the report is written, so is the executive summary. Some people, however, like to write the executive summary when they start out, using it as a guide or outline for putting the plan together. It is then revised as you go along. In any event, it can only be finalized after the plan is written.

Some people only read executive summaries, so you have to get across the full impact of the plan in the executive summary. It should contain sufficient information to stand on its own but not be of great detail.

The Executive Summary usually serves the following purposes:

- Defines the organization
- States the vision
- Describes the mission
- Includes a situational analysis
- Lists the goals
- Lays out the strategies
- Provides financial information
- Indicates who will be responsible for what
- Sets the milestones

It also includes why, when, and how things will happen.

Executive Summary A brief outline of the essential and key points of your plan.

LIST OF ACRONYMS

If a goodly number of acronyms are used then it is wise to list them at the beginning of the report. If there are only a few, they can be defined within the report. A moderate number can be listed in the appendix.

Acronym A word made from the first initials of a series of words. For example, *Voice Of Customer* would be *VOC*.

Introduction and Preface

Some plan-writers like to have an Introduction and/or a Preface. There is no set usage or prescribed way of using an Introduction or a Preface. I like to use one or the other to clearly state the purpose of the plan and acknowledge the people who were involved in developing it. It is purely a personal choice whether to use them or not.

Situational Analysis

A situational analysis is often put into the written plan to give the readers a clear idea of the organization's present situation. It contains a competitive and/or external environment analysis in relation to the internal situation of the company.

In some instances the SWOT analysis, research, or some other analysis is incorporated into the body of the plan. Personally, I like to see the situational analysis, which draws conclusions from the various analyses, in the body of the plan and things like the SWOT analysis, research details, and other analyses in the appendix. (See Lesson 13 for a full discussion of the Situational Analysis.)

Key Findings and Conclusions

In this section you list the findings of your research and analysis and the conclusions you have drawn from these findings. The section not only reveals what you have learned, but it establishes the *raison d'être* of your plan.

Raison d'être The reason that something exists.

Recommendations

From the findings and conclusions you have drawn, you should now be able to list your Goals and Strategies (what your aims are and how you will accomplish them). Along with spelling out the goals and strategies, it is a good idea to include a schedule, or at least the milestones and who will be responsible for accomplishing them. A detailed schedule can be included in the appendix.

You should also indicate in your recommendations how you will monitor and measure the steps to achieve your goals. Some people like to have a separate section for monitoring and measuring.

Budgets and Financial Projections

The amount of financial information or the complexity of the budget depends on what you are planning for. Key financial or budget information is usually in the body of the plan with back up materials in the appendix.

SUPPORT DOCUMENTS, GLOSSARY, AND BACKUP MATERIAL

Most written plans have a section called the *Appendix* that contains additional details and documents that support the plan. The Appendix can house reference materials, a glossary, exhibits, charts, detailed backup material, brochures, financial charts, and any other items that support the plan.

MISCELLANEOUS SECTION TOPICS

Here is a list of a variety of possible topics or sections that you might want to include in your plan.

Advertising and Promotion

Business Relationships

Competition

Customers

Distribution

Management

Manufacturing

Market Analysis

Marketing Strategy

Pricing and Profitability

Production

Products/Services Description

Public Relations

Research

Risk Analysis

Sales

Use of funding proceeds

The list is not all inclusive and is offered only to trigger ideas for writing your plan.

Circular, Not Linear The written plan is the culmination of the planning process. Don't forget, however, that the process is circular and must be constantly monitored, measured, and re-visited.

In this lesson you learned about the content of the written plan, the form it should take, questions to determine the form, how the plan comes together, and writing the plan.

INDEX

SYMBOLS

A

B

C

D

E

F

G

I-K

L

M

N-O

P

Q

R

S

T

V

W